THE COUNTRY GUIDE

GUIDE

FOR CITY PEOPLE

THE COUNTRY GUIDE

FOR CITY PEOPLE

CHASE COLLINS

STEIN AND DAY/*Publishers*/**New York**

First published in 1973
Copyright © 1973 by Chase Collins
Library of Congress Catalog Card No. 73-79798
All rights reserved
Published simultaneously in Canada by Saunders of Toronto, Ltd.
Designed by David Miller
Printed in the United States of America
Stein and Day/*Publishers*/Scarborough House, Briarcliff Manor, New York 10510
ISBN 0–8128–1610–2

To the Pickle Maker

CONTENTS

About five years ago city life really got to me. I decided
I had to get in touch with the country, with fresh air, open
spaces, trees, and silence, so I began looking for a place
where I could find them. At the time I thought there would
be nothing to it. But, because I was raised in an urban
area, I really knew very little about rural customs, attitudes,
and property. What little I thought I knew was the result
of stereotypes, storybooks, and second-hand information.

Since then I've learned a lot. Sure, rural America is
full of green places where you can live more gently, work
with your hands, and let your mind wander. But buying
land in the country isn't simple. The rural real estate market
is rather sophisticated.

That's why I wrote this book. It's full of the experience
I've had and the things I've learned. I'll tell you about
some of the different ways to look for land and how not
to look for it. I'll spend some time explaining the various
ways land is sold and what affects its price. I have some
ideas for you on how to shorten your search and enjoy
it more, along with tips on country lenders, money matters,
and legal things you'll have to consider. I'll be talking
about old houses, their joys and pitfalls, and I'll spend

some time on farm facts that'll make it easier for you to talk to your neighbor and not sound like a slicker who doesn't know beans.

There's more too. Introductions to people you're likely to have as friends and help through early country difficulties. It's a happy book from a happy person. I hope you like it. And I hope it'll make your search a successful one.

THE COUNTRY GUIDE

FOR CITY PEOPLE

1

THE BEGINNING

Maybe you think you know what you want in the country. I can guess what it is since it's probably what I wanted. You want to have enough land to walk around on, some trees, and a neighbor who is a mile away but still cordial when he sees you. You want some land for a garden. You want privacy, and the house can't be some new ranch-style thing. You want to build a shelter yourself, or find an old farmhouse you can fix up. You want to see animals poking around, you want to see stars and hear crickets.

Perfect. So much for the commonplace. You'll find every one of these things in the country. That's what the country is: trees, grass, land, gardens, crickets, and stars. A breeze blowing through your solitude.

Making the decision to start looking for a place in the country is so full of hurrahs that it will take you a while to settle down. You'll keep thinking about herbs and hammocks and summer days; you'll fantasize when you should be doing some grown-up thinking.

I'll never be the one to pooh-pooh fantasy and dreaming, but dreaming isn't going to get you to the farm. You've got to start thinking about it differently, because next to your sunlit enthusiasms some solid planning will determine whether or not you make it happily to that land and how fast you do it. Don't go off wandering the countryside with only hammocks and sweet basil on your mind, because you'll end up going in circles. You'll waste time looking at things you should have known were out of the question. You'll waste your feelings on fantastic places you can't afford or, even worse, fall in love with something you cannot take care of.

Before you get in the car and open your map, before you do anything, decide what you want and what you can pay for it. That's the first step.

As long as it's not simply to get out of the city, the other reasons why you are looking should help you to set out the criteria for your place in the country. For instance, you might want a subsistence farm, one that supplies you with everything you need—all your food and all the raw materials for shelter, clothing, furniture, and heat, plus a small income. Clearly, if this is the kind of life you want, your needs in land will be different from those of the person who intends to raise one product on his land and purchase all the rest of what he needs with the income from this specialty. And different again from the needs of the person who wants to raise a few chickens, four trout, three oak trees, vegetables, one hog, and an apple tree and try to sell all of them at a profit. Every purpose calls for different kinds and amounts of land. You may decide you want to live on the farm but not count on it as your only source of income. By raising a basementful of mushrooms and also working a job in a nearby town, you may find the kind of peace and security you want. But again, your land needs will be different from those of the subsistence farmer, the specialty people, or the general farmer.

If you want a farm that balances your urban life, the

Different kinds of apple trees should be mixed together. Because, in order for most trees to produce, they have to cross-pollinate with another apple variety. Pollination happens when the tree is in bloom and bees help the trees get together.

kind of place you go to on weekends after working in the big city, you are free to choose the esthetic over the practical, but you're more restricted in the total area you can choose from because it has to be within driving distance of the big city. Also, you'll have to consider the problem of leaving the house alone for days, with the greater risk of fire and theft and having the furnace break down in January. But even these considerations pale when you remember that for a few days a week at least, you don't have to bolt your door three times, you can take a midnight walk if you want to, and you don't have to worry about someone ripping off your car while you buy your groceries.

But back to the point. After you've figured out what you plan to do with the land, the criteria for your place will become quite specific. You'll know exactly what you want and can then start looking for the land that fits your needs.

To help you get started, here is a list of questions to answer before you make your first trip.

1. How much land do you want or need?
2. Does the land have to have certain soil conditions?
3. Do you want woods on the land?
4. A pond or stream?
5. How should the land look? Smooth or hilly?
6. Do you want bare land or land with buildings?
7. How far can your farm be from the town or market?
8. How far can your farm be from the big city if you plan to drive there on weekends?
9. How much cash do you have for a down payment and closing costs?
10. Would you rather pay cash for the entire purchase price, or will you need to finance part of it?

Twilight is traveling
time for animals,
especially deer.

11. Will you have additional money to make required repairs?

12. Do you want to buy a livable house or would you like to build?

13. Must the house have indoor plumbing? If it doesn't, are you willing to put it in?

14. Do you want central heating?

15. How much repair work can you do yourself? (Plumbing, electrical, and roofing as well as general fixing.)

16. Do you need any other buildings on the land?

17. Do you want a private road to ensure your feeling of privacy?

2

WAYS TO LOOK FOR LAND

STARTING THE SEARCH

Weekends will probably be your time to look, but don't count on finding and buying the place in a few weekends or less. The old-fashioned happy ending comes after patience and a lot of work, and the place that fits your requirements and your pocket may take a while. It took us four months.

A good first step is an unstructured, back-road drive through the part of the state you're interested in. It could be done in a few weekends if you keep moving most of the time. This way you can get an overview of the possibilities in the state, the lay of the land in different areas, and a feeling for towns and their people. Naturally, you won't pick up details on these weekends, but you will find yourself primarily attracted to one or two areas. At this point, you could begin to concentrate your search in the three or four counties that attract you by calling the telephone company in the county seat and getting a telephone book. This will give you names of people that will help you: real estate agents, bankers, agricultural agents, and a lot of other country contacts. The following weekend you can begin your search in earnest and particular.

Maps

A road map can do more for you than tell you how to get from place to place. By looking at the way the roads are laid out, straight or curvy, you can get a rough topographical reading of the state. Hilly areas will have winding roads because the road builders like to take the path of least resistance, and that means going around rather than over. Often the road hugs the sides of hills because a low valley road will be muddy when it rains. Flat land inspires clean right angles, long ruler-straight stretches of road. A careful look at your road map can tell you how the earth moves.

If you really want to know details of elevation and other topographical features, you can send for topographical maps from the U.S. Geographical Survey. These maps are cheap and you can order them by state, even by specific areas within a state if you want to. Send for an index of maps or a specific state.

Map Information Service
U. S. Geological Survey
Department of Interior
Washington, D.C. 20240

Once you've really narrowed your area of search, another kind of map will help you. It's called a plat book, and it contains a series of maps covering at least the whole county. On page after page, the country's smaller secret places are set out for you: places and things you'll never see on a road map, and maybe miss even if you actually drive by them. On the maps you'll see the boundries between farms, what the owner's name is, and how much land is his. You'll see streams, rivers, and roads. Little dots on the plat maps indicate where the house is located on the land. If you are looking for an abandoned house, you'll be able to see that one owner may have two or three houses shown on the land he owns. He can probably use only one, so you could look him up; you've got all the roads indicated and can get there easily. Don't tell him you saw his name in a plat book, by the way. I think plat books get pretty close to being Peeping Toms and should be used politely by anyone who has one.

Getting a plat book is simple. Go to a real estate agent in the county you like and ask to see his. Somewhere in the book the publisher's name and address will be printed. Remember the source and send them a letter requesting the book for the county you're interested in. They may run two dollars or so, depending on the publisher. Get one or two; they are very informative.

A FEW PERSONAL THINGS

Ford and Chevy are the main types of cars in the country, and if you pull up in your super different car you may feel like an outsider. You can't help the car, but you can lessen the impression of city sharpie by dressing casually. A suit is out, flashy-cosmopolitan outfits are out. The obvious no-bra look is out. Be sure to wear field-type shoes if you want to look at land. Use common sense; the less attention you call to your cityness, the better.

Some towns won't notice your long hair; they've got their own freaky-looking kids running around wearing fatigues and tennis shoes. In other places you're a freak if you come into town at all because they know everyone that ever comes into town and you're not one of them.

If you're thirsty for an orange juice or a beer some afternoon and are sensitive to hassles, the town bar is the main place to avoid. Sometimes it can get a little surly in there. It all depends on the town.

A real estate office is not exactly a welcome wagon for freaks. The salesman there, like anywhere else, may be a little scared of you—may have some strong opinion about your hygiene and definitely would rather spend his time with someone who looks like he has money to spend and to pay commissions with. Besides these predictable irritations, there's no one in the country who's going to fiddle with your head because of the hair that's there.

No matter who you are, the main thing to do with your mouth is smile. A smile diminishes barriers, age differences, and the country myth that city people are grim snobs. You'll probably find that smiling comes easy, because you're out of the city, talking to pretty friendly people and loving the whole idea. You can't help it—you smile.

The other thing to do with your mouth is to keep words like "hick," "dope," "shit," "fuck," and "swimming pool" out of it. They are not appreciated by country people. Use them when you're alone. Naturally, there are subjects to avoid too, at least at the outset. Debate over chemical fertilizers is one, food prices is another, your political opinions another. Keep them to yourself until you know who you are talking to.

BIG NUMBERS LAND AND HOW TO AVOID IT

To find inexpensive land you should remember one thing: the seller will charge what the market will bear. If the price is out of line, no one will buy; if the price is reasonable to one person, the price will be met and become a precedent. Okay. You are not the only one who wants out of the

city. Many others, with a lot more money than you, are out there looking too. Your ace is to figure out what "they" want and avoid it.

Specifically, there are several things that are going to increase the price of any place in the country. Every one of them you can do without and not suffer. Here they are.

1. Proximity to a major city. The closer you get to any city, even a smaller one, the higher the price of the land. Close in, you're paying extra for the convenience of being right next door to a pizza parlor and its blinking sign. You're paying extra for the convenience of a short trip to the city and for the possible future value of the land as a chromy suburb. If you want to get out of the city, get out of the city. It's that simple. Get twenty miles out, fifty miles out, a hundred miles out, depending on the size and appetites of the city. Get way way way way out and pay less money for more privacy, peace, and silence.

2. Major highways and freeways. The closeness of transportation routes directly affects the "value" of the land. Life is more convenient the closer you are to a big road, and a lot of people pay a lot of money for that. You may not need it. If you don't, avoid the noise and intrusion that come with convenience, and pay less—get off the road.

3. Development projects. Sometimes development projects are well conceived, planned, and beautifully executed. They often include a good sized lake. Other times developments are the ones that take some stinking hole that nobody could do anything with, fill it in, set up come-on pony rides for the kiddies, stake it off in fifteen-foot lots worth their weight in diamonds, and call the whole shot some fantasy name. Get yourself in one of these and you're sur-

rounded with seven million vacationing city people who are getting back to basics with the help of their electric hibachis.

Later in the chapter I'll go into some details on buying development land, but for now it's enough to say that development land tends to be expensive, maybe just a little cheaper than going city prices, but a lot more than current country land values. But that's not the only problem. Country communities that have developments nearby are usually pretty delighted to have so many new taxable properties, and they tax 'em good. After all, city people with second homes have a lot more disposable income and it might just as well be spent on the community's schools, road maintenance or whatever. A little secluded tract a few miles away won't have taxes like the development does, and it'll be cheaper to begin with.

4. Water. If there's a good spring, a creek, pond, river, or lake on the land, the land will be more expensive. The farmer, especially the one who raises animals, is willing to pay more for land that has water on it because his animals require it. And if the pond or spring is in the pasture area, he doesn't have to rig up a trough and water system. Nature has done his work for him. The city buyer has other reasons for wanting water, the main one being the beauty of it. It's poetic, it's restful, and it fits the fantasies we have about country things.

Water, no matter what the source, is important to the value of the land, no matter who is buying. But the city buyer is often willing to pay even more for the realization of fantasy and the sellers in the country know it. You have to decide just how much you can pay for an emotional thing. Sometimes, even if it costs a lot, it's worth it.

It could be cheaper to buy land with pond potential (good springs) rather than pay the high price for an existing one.

HOW LAND IS PRICED

One of the most basic things to remember about country property is that it is sold by the acre. $100 an acre, $500 an acre, whatever; the price is quoted on a per acre basis. This is confusing to a city person. We don't know exactly how big an acre is—and we buy houses, not acres, in the city.

To put your mind at ease, the per acre price on improved land, that is land with buildings, includes basically three things. 1. The value of the buildings: the house and its comforts, the barn and its age and capabilities, plus the various outbuildings. 2. The value of the land as farmland: the quality of the soil, the availability of water, lay of the land (flat is better for crops) and the percentage of tillable acres. Timber, if any, is also included in the price. 3. And the newest addition, as far as you are concerned: the aesthetic value of the land. Sometimes this feature is the big expense in recreational land. Long rolling hills, deep forests, marshes growing cat tails are lovely things and you will most likely be willing to pay much more for them than a farmer would.

When you look at improved land, keep these things in mind. They'll make your comparison shopping easier.

ABANDONED FARMS AND COUNTRY RUMORS

Abandoned farms don't cost much. And you should know the reasons why before you buy one. This isn't to say that an abandoned farm is a bad buy, it's just that a rambling scrambling little place may be a bad buy for you. And you have to be the judge.

Abandoned farms are cheap because they're sometimes

gritty places. The land on the farm may be hostile to plants and growing, or it may be devastatingly flooded every few years; it may be eroded past redemption because the owner didn't or couldn't take care of it. And with the land shot, the owner was forced to leave; as farmland it was worthless.

The question to ask now is, Worthless to whom? Maybe your plans won't be hampered by land that's been hacked by the elements or bad farming practices. It's possible the problem with the land can be corrected with intensive care and money. There's no such thing as worthless land. It is just worthless for certain purposes.

The biggest reason why farms are abandoned has to do with that old grabber, economics. The self-sustaining family farm, the apple orchard life we read about in high school, doesn't exist much any more. A couple of chickens, a peach tree, one hog, and a huge garden just can't make it. True, the old concept of self-sufficiency has been altered and updated by many young people today with some success, but not necessarily financial success. They have managed in fact to get around the idea that money equals survival. Unfortunately, their philosophy is shared by very few. The farmer today, like every other businessman, is out there punching the clock with his new green $10,000 machine, and comes back at the end of the day (sometimes as late as ten at night) to a barn loaded with more special equipment that may have cost him $100,000. He's in debt up to his ears, will be in debt till he retires, and he's fighting for every dime he makes. He's in a tough market and he has to be efficient, smart, and aggressive. If he wants to make money, he doesn't do much whittling, doesn't fool around making music or writing books. He's got bills to pay.

Big business down on the farm has put a lot of little guys, unwilling or unable to match the competition dollar for dollar, method for method, out on the streets. And when the end is near, the money gone, it's sometimes just easier to pack a few things and leave the farm.

Whether the sad cause is economic, philosophic, or old-fashioned incompetence on the farmer's part, the farm is abandoned to the weather and small animals. The grasses grow, things get wilder, and one day, if the poor farmer's luck changes, his old neighbor gets in touch with him, the one who's succeeding in his operation and is always looking to expand. He offers to buy the acreage for a small price. He says he plans to start revamping the land, put in a new pasture, plant trees, any number of things, maybe use a couple of the outbuildings to store his machines. No, he doesn't plan to use the house, maybe he'll tear it down.

The owner sells gladly, but seldom does the new owner get around to tearing down the old house. It just sits there, empty, while the farmer gets at his new land.

So, there sits the house till you drive by. You see the broken windows, rainy curtains, tall burry weeds and overgrown driveway. You look around from a distance, no one's there, no one's across the road looking at you, so you walk up to the house.

Go inside carefully; if the place is in shreds, you might fall through the floor. Watch it. If there's been a fire, stay out. With luck, though, the house will be good and you can have an eerie tour through the rooms, the discards, and the rubble. There's a kind of hum in an abandoned house; the silence of old flowered wallpaper, torn mattresses, 1962 *Life* magazines, pictures of little girls carrying ducklings to water that have bird dirt on their frames. Bumblebees flying around a torn screen door. I am a lover of underdogs. This sad old place would be a good home for people that can love it, fix it, and keep it warm and dry.

An underdog is one thing; a lovable loser is another. Learn how to spot a loser. Check to see that the foundation is solid, make sure the rain hasn't rotted the wooden skeleton, and read chapter 4 on how to judge the old thing. It's romantic to think you can save this old dreamer, but it's stupid sentimentality to pour yourself and your money into it and have it reward you with collapse. You can't save a house that's not solid; or maybe I should say you might as well build from scratch.

If you think you've found a good one, the logical next step is to drive over to the neighboring farm and ask some questions. It's likely that when the place went wild, this guy bought it and now uses the land and buildings. Drive in slowly. They have no idea who you are. Get out of your car, smile, greet them, and say you noticed the empty place next door and do they know who owns the land. They'll probably know and they'll tell you if they like you. They can give you the owner's name and a clue on how to reach him, or they'll say it belongs to them. Now you mention that you're looking for a place in the area and if it's theirs would they consider selling the house and some land to you. If you want a small bit of land, up to ten acres or so, you may find the owner's a seller.

Your suggestion may make some sense to the owner because he pays taxes on the old farm and he pays more taxes if there are buildings on it. Buildings are an improvement on the land and real estate taxes are based in good part on how the land has been improved. If the unused buildings (the house, etc.) were gone, the owner wouldn't have such high taxes. That's why farmers sometimes toss a couple of gallons of gasoline on old unused buildings and drop a burning thing or two in the gas. The buildings are gone, the taxes are lower.

Valleys are good and bad as garden spots. Cold air will sink into a valley and may harm your plants. Water will gather there too. But often the valley soil is the richest because it is made of top soil that's been washed off the hillsides.

In the same way, if the farmer didn't happen to own that small bit of land that has buildings on it, he could accomplish the same thing: lower taxes. He'd be left with the land he'd originally bought the place for, and he wouldn't have the buildings that he doesn't want anyhow. And you'd have a house and some acreage.

What a sales pitch! It's perfect: you help him, he helps you. Everybody is happy.

If, however, this great number doesn't interest him for one reason or another, that's okay. Be nice about it and ask him if there's any other place around that he thinks could be bought. He may know of places that real estate agents haven't listed. If he tells you about any, check them out. He may tell you the rumor that Emil Pec down in Five Mile Creek is thinking about selling, and if you're smart as well as curious, you'll try to locate the old man.

Emil Pec isn't listed in the phone book in Five Mile Creek. It turns out he's been living in a town nearby for the last three years, so you and your friend get his address and go over, knock on his front door, and listen to the radio playing inside. No one answers. You look around the yard. The grass is dry and old Pec has some funny-looking plastic bottles stuck on sticks in the ground. The bottles have been cut into lacy patterns and they swing and whistle in the breeze. It's July and Pec doesn't seem to be around.

"He's out in Five Mile Creek," a neighbor yells. "Ya lookin' for Pec?"

"Yes," you say.

"Farm's out on Country O. He's probably out there."

"Okay, thanks a lot."

You drive out again to Five Mile Creek, taking curvy Country O until you come to a milk can with a mailbox stuck in it marked Pec. The road into Pec's farm is marked by four more whirling detergent bottles, so you know you've found the right place. The dust settles as you stop your car next to a '51 Ford truck and look around for signs of life. Insects buzz. The sun shines on a small brick house with a big pine tree by the door. The land is pretty. You're getting out of your car when a voice comes from inside the old truck.

"Who are ya?"

"Mr. Pec? Hello . . . ah . . . we, we heard you were selling this place, Mr. Pec, and we wanted to see you about it. Is that true?"

Very slowly he rolls the truck window down; it squeaks. He leans out to look at you. His face looks like a crumpled paper bag, his light-blue eyes have been bleached by sixty years of farm sun.

"You farmers?" he says, looking at your tennis shoes. If you're tempted to say yes, forget it. He knows who you are. It's written all over you and your Red Ball Jets.

"You want a tour?" says Mr. Pec, "I guess I kin give ya a tour if you're interested."

After several violent yanks on the handle, Pec gets the truck door open, lifts his left leg with both hands, sets it on the running board, and, holding onto the steering wheel, lowers himself onto two feet. Pause. Breathe, breathe. Then he adjusts his blue stripped hat down over his eyebrows, grabs the strap of his overalls, and begins giving you the tour of your life. The fish pond is the first stop.

"There's two thousand trouts in there," he says, pointing at a blue pond, set amid grassy banks, that you'd run to if it weren't for him hobbling next to you. "Trouts in there're 'bout three pounds each. And that's the baby pond over there. That's where the baby trouts is."

"Hmmmmmmm," you say, shaking your head.

"Had a robb'ry here last week," he continues. "They came in and robbed me outa five hundred pounds of fish. Come at night and just took 'em right out. Didn't hear a thing. Mighta been hippies done it."

You fiddle with your hair and say, "Terrible, isn't that a shame."

"All that water's spring water, ya know, comes right in the pond from a spring . . . 'bout two hundred gallons a minute, and drains out over there." He points at a trickling little stream you hadn't seen till now.

"Gee, beautiful." You wonder if they say "gee" in the country. You said it to give that "harmless innocent" impression. You want him to like you.

Emil Pec digs into a big pocket of his overalls and gives you a handful of stuff that looks like rabbit droppings and pours it in your hand—fish food. And when you throw it in the pond, the fish go crazy. An incredible splashing, jumping, flopping, swishing goes on. You start jumping up and down and clapping your hands as Mr. Pec picks up a rusty rake from the deep grass, leans on it, and waits for you to calm down.

He looks silently out over the fields for a while then says, "Out there's ninety acres of the best farmin' land in the county. Why, people've offered to give me a lot of money for it, but I wouldn't sell. Riches' land around, but I wouldn't sell."

"How come?" you say.

Pec squints. Looks away from you. "Had a man here from New York City once, said he'd give ten thousand dollars for that land. But I had a family then. There's a daughter now living in Milwaukee. A dental technician.

She's got three kids. Ten, eight, an' seven. Boy's a real genius. Skipped two grades already."

And you listen to fifteen minutes of talk about his daughter, the kids, Milwaukee, the genius, and lots of other things while you look out at the richest land in the county. You're listening with one ear and trying with your whole head to see how this land looks any different from any of the other land around there. It just doesn't look any different to you. Ten thousand dollars? There's trees, pasture, weeds, just like everywhere else. This is the richest land around?

"Had cows in here a couple a months ago," Emil Pec continues as you walk down a little hill. "Best pasture's right here. See that grass? That's real good pasture grass. Kept twenty head fat and happy right here. Not many pastures that size can take twenty cows."

"Did you sell them?" you ask.

"Yep. Gettin' too old," he says slowly, "Couldn't take care of 'em right. But I got a good price for 'em, that's for sure. Good price." And you look out at that pasture grass to see how it's different from other pastures. You notice there's not a cow plop for miles, and you wonder if it's really been just two months since the cows.

"Over there's the melon patch," he goes on, nodding at a crawling mass of leaves and yellow trumpet flowers, "And there's strawberries here. Quats of 'em. Quats and quats of the reddes' bigges' berries ya ever seen. An' these maple trees—"

"Those are maples, huh?"

"Yeah," he says, looking at you sideways, as though you're even greener than he'd thought, "these maples give sugar so fast in the spring I hired three boys just to carry the pails in. One tree'd fill a pail before ya had time to

Cow needs:

1. 2 acres of pasture.
2. a milking twice a day, once in the morning, once at night.
3. gentle handling.
4. twenty pounds of hay a day.
5. ten-twenty pounds of grain.
6. an equal amount of water, especially on hot summer days.

empty the first one. You know how much money ya can get for sugarin'?''

"No, how much?"

"A lot. Make a lot of money on maple trees. Specially these." And he lets that really sink in. You stand in the shade of the maples, surrounded by strawberries, melons, yellow flowers, and the million different greens of summertime and look at your best friend.

"What're these trees, Mr. Pec?" You ask quietly.

"Well, those're plum. All them's plum. Y' get bushels o' plums every fall off of these trees. Big juicy ones that jus' fall off into your hand. Darn good, too, if you like plums. Ya could sell 'em."

Moving slowly through the long good-smelling grass up toward the house, Pec says, "You folks ever seen a grapevine? That's one there. See that big overgrown fence, that's grapes. Go on over. The reason it's so bushy is that it's got so many grapes I have to give 'em away. Go see em. They're just coming out now." You go over, of course.

"These green things, Mr. Pec?" you yell.

"Yeah, that's grapes."

"Hey, look at this, babe, look at these grapes. Fantastic. They're all over the place. Come here, honey, come look at these grapes!" You can't control yourself. You bit down on the hard little bunch in your hand and spit the sour things out. "It's really grapes!"

"Yep," says Pec as you come bounding back down to him, catch your breath, and tell him it's really a nice farm he's got here. "Yep," says Pec, it's a good farm all right, that's why I call it my little gold mine. It's just my little gold mine." He looks around.

The phrase hangs in the air like a balloon as you all

walk towards the house, past the peony patch and the unkempt roses and up onto the old wooden porch. No screens.

Inside the house the sun pouring through all the windows almost makes the rooms wiggle. A pump in the kitchen, but no refrigerator that you can see. Old stained woodwork around the doors, a big black metal heat stove in the living-room with a pipe that runs from it to the wall above. The rooms are small with a kind of ratty carpeting on the floor and boxes are stacked in one corner along with two jars of homemade pickles. The stairs to the second floor are almost vertical, and the two bare bedrooms upstairs have A shaped ceilings.

Pec waits downstairs for you, and when you come back down, you walk over to a window to see the view. Before you touch the sash Pec says he just finished painting all the rooms and you won't be able to open the window. Painted all the windows shut, but a screwdriver'd open 'em easy, he says. So what if the windows don't open, you can fix that. Strange it doesn't smell like fresh paint and the rooms don't look all that clean.

So what.

You love the place. You can't help it. It's such a neat little—what's the word?—gold mine. Spiritual gold mine.

The two of you walk down the stairs and outside ahead of Emil Pec and exchange looks. Do you like it? Yes. Do you? Yes!

Then up comes Pec behind you.

"How much are you selling the place for, Mr. Pec?"

Well. Mr. Pec doesn't know exactly. "There's awful good land out here," he says. "Good pasture. Good trees. Good farmland. Nice little house. And I built the barn, myself. Ya can make a lot of money on this place. That's if yer smart . . . and good with yer hands. You folks handy?''

"Yes," you nod and smile and nod and smile.

"Me too. Why I made them little wind machines myself,'' he says pointing to the plastic bottles whirling on their sticks in the grass, "Sold 'em for three dollars a piece. People'd give me money for 'em and give 'em away for Christmas presents.''

"Yes, but—''

"Know what they are? Why, they're nothin but soap bottles. Empty soap bottles. And I cut 'em out like that, so they'd whistle. One Christmas we had so much snow up here, they'd be writin' me letters just to get a couple of them toys—''

"Well, Mr. Pec," you interrupt, "we like the place. So we thought, maybe we could give you a down payment and work out the details—''

"Maybe," says the old man rubbing his chin and hobbling towards the truck again while you walk along beside him, getting in each other's way. "But I might have an offer now from a man in Chicago's got three kids . . . for fifteen thousand." You swallow. The offer's high. "Supposed to get a letter from him today . . . that's why I'm out here," says Pec. "As a matter of fact, he's got three kids just like me and my wife did. She's dead now. Died in March '69. A good person she was. Born jus' four miles from here, in a town called Viola. Ya know it?''

"No, but maybe we'll drive over there sometime. When do you think you might hear from this guy in Chicago? Is the farm definitely sold?''

"Well, that sorta depends on the letter don't it? Yes.

And no. The farm ain't sold just yet. Might be." And he pulls himself into the truck and closes the door. You both lean over to see him through the window. "You folks got any kids?"

"No, we don't, Mr. Pec. But—"

"That's too bad. Now I got three kids myself. Two boys and a girl. The oldes' boy's a electrician over in Ada. You folks farmers?"

"No sir, we're not, but—we'd like to buy your farm, it's a beautiful place, you know that yourself. Seems to have all the things we've been looking for, and, if the price is right, we'd like to move in this fall sometime. What do you think? How much do you want for it?"

"This fall, huh. That's no time to start farmin'. Why, this place freezes up so fast you won't get nothin' done 'fore winter. Gets cold up here, you know. That stove o' mine'll keep you plenty warm, if ya know how to work it—probab'ly don't know, tho. That stove's kept me and mine warm all the winters we had up here. I remember September '41 we got twenty-four inches 'fore I even got the corn in. Now that's unusual, but, let's see, could a been five years ago, I'd been out hayin' when up there over that ridge comes the meanest storm I ever seen in my whole life . . ."

And so it goes for another ten minutes or so, until you finally start your car and leave, never getting an answer to how much Mr. Pec wants for his little gold mine. Or whether it's even for sale or already sold.

This is the very old story of what a rumor can do to you. If you have the luck to run into an old salesman like Emil Pec who leads you through his country garden, tells you about his family, sells you his melon patch and brick house and pond, you can end up pretty disappointed.

Once in a while, an old man like Pec will start talk that he's going to sell, because he probably should sell. He's alone now. But in his heart he can't stand the thought of it. So, one summer afternoon you appear at his lonely old truck, ask about his farm, and he's off and hobbling; telling you all the joys of the place, exaggerating them, petting them, reliving his memories, overjoyed that you're there to listen. And his farm is all the more valuable to his old heart if you actually want to own the place yourself and make him an offer on the spot.

Don't hesitate to chase a rumor all over the country, but when you're face to face with a fantastic little farm and Emil Pec—forget it. Half of what made it so fine was listening to him tell you about it.

THE REAL ESTATE MAN

Most country land is sold through real estate men. Not all of it, of course, because a good deal of buying and selling goes on between neighbors who have adjoining property, and there are numerous other ways to contact sellers, many of which I'll be talking about later in the book.

The real estate man is a human being. Yes, it's true. He has a heart and hands and all that makes us up, but he's not perfect. If you are lucky you'll meet a real estate man who is good; otherwise you may have to put up with some indifference to you and your plans.

We found that the biggest problem with rural real estate men was that they didn't listen awfully well. They seldom called us back to tell us about a new listing they thought we'd like. Consequently, we spun our wheels a lot trying to keep up with new farms for sale in all the parts of the

Put signs up.

state we were interested in. We couldn't do the job efficiently, naturally, and probably missed quite a few nice ones. If we'd made friends with a good agent we could have saved ourselves a lot of gas and frustration. We learned that real estate sales methods in the country are not quite as efficient as they are in the city.

After several contacts with real estate men, maybe three months' worth, off and on, we discovered something. Although we thought just going into an office was sufficient to tell the agent we were truly interested in buying, we found ourselves forced to tell him clearly and with quotations of figures, that we wanted to buy, were ready to buy, and had the money to buy. If you plan to work through an agent, tell him sincerely and honestly what you want, how much you can spend, and, if you get the chance, that you would like to have him call or write you on new listings. If he hems and haws, go somewhere else. It is important that he realize you mean business. Also, be certain to contact all the agents in the area that you are interested in. They all have different listings and rarely do they cooperate with each other as city real estate people do.

Real estate offices are open on weekends—that's when they do much of their business. You can stop in just about anytime and find someone there, but if you are really serious about an area, give a couple of different agents a call or send a letter telling them when you're going to be there and that you would like to arrange a time to meet, talk, and see a few of their listings.

Once you're there, if he has something to show you, the real estate man will drive you around all day if you want to. During the drive you can learn great and little country things. You can see miles of the area without spending a penny on gasoline and get a running commentary at every turn. You will be driven up and down the county, taking beautiful shortcuts to pieces of land for sale; sit back and see how the land looks, how the trees look; you can count the bridges you cross and roughly figure out how many streams are trickling through those fields. You can cover a lot of ground and have a nice time asking the man questions. If you're lucky, he's the talkative type and he'll tell you about the crops that are growing, the last natural disaster in the area, where the good farmland is, what the people are like, and anything else that comes up. By the way, he rarely hesitates to wear his prejudices on his sleeve, and carrying a sign wouldn't make him much clearer. Don't feel you must convert him to your point of view; keep quiet and get your work done or, if you can't stand it, see someone else; he's definitely not the only agent in town.

As you're driving on little country roads, you'll notice that every time you pass trucks, cars, tractors, wagons, kids, or dogs, the real estate man will lift one finger from the steering wheel. That's a wave. And although there are local variations in the delivery, it's a common thing. His country wave doesn't necessarily mean that he knows the people he waves at or that they know him when they wave back. It's just that when a car goes by on one of these far-out roads it's an occasion. It's contact, so you wave; you all wave. It's beautiful.

When a real estate man lists a piece of land, he and the seller sit down and talk about money. The seller says he wants $200 million for it; the agent says it can't be sold at that price, but let's try to keep it as high as possible. Finally they agree on a slightly inflated price and wait for you to come along. Since the price is based on the emotions, investments, and needs of the seller as well as the opinion of the real estate broker, you're going to find some variation

when you see geese
it's spring for sure -
robins get fooled
sometimes and
get caught in
cold weather.

in pricing. Equal pieces of land will have different prices. Get to know what's fair in the area you like. And the simplest way to compare prices is to figure out what each place costs per acre. If you learn one area is pricing land at, say, $300 an acre generally, find out why one or two farms feel theirs is worth $450. Maybe there's a reason. Maybe the land is much richer, or the house is in better condition. Remember that farmland and the house and other buildings on it are not sold separately, but at a total price per acre.

If you buy a piece of land that the real estate man shows you, he gets a commission. Usually about 5 to 8 per cent of the sale price. This commission is technically paid by the person who sells the farm to you, but don't forget that the seller has tacked this cost onto the actual price he wants to have in his pocket when he leaves the place. So in fact, you end up paying the real estate man.

Sometimes, even often, his help has been worth the commission. The broker has steered you toward the land you want, he has done the negotiating with the seller for you, and he often offers to help you find financing, insurance, a lawyer, or any number of other things you might need.

If you decide to look for land through a real estate broker, you should expect him to give you good service, keep your discussions about money to himself, and inform you of any red tape you might encounter. And while we're on the subject of expectations, the broker should expect you to be straight with him about what you're really looking for, and how much money you are willing and able to spend; he'll expect you to let him do all the negotiating with the seller.

THE FANTASY CATALOG

You and your shiny new realty company catalog can cover thousands of miles without starting an engine, spending one cent, or getting lost. If you don't know where you're going, get a catalog.

Several of the larger national realty companies put out a compendium of juicy places they have for sale all over the country. Each local office of the company sends a picture and write-up of a few of its favorite listings, then they put the book together, advertise its existence in everything from the *Wall Street Journal* to *Hoard's Dairyman*, and mail out copies to interested people.

When you are looking at a catalog, you are not seeing all the listings the company has—just the local favorites. I call them favorites because I don't think the word "best" applies. The listings tend to be expensive, glamorous, or out of the ordinary, with a few regulars thrown in for sake of reality. You'll see blurbs about mountain cabins in virgin forest for sale. You'll see chrome and redwood creations, and rustic sun-weathered farmhouses looking at themselves in half-mile river frontages. You'll see every fantasy you ever had and then some.

The problem with catalogs is that you always see something you absolutely must have. You find it hard to believe anyone in his right mind would want to sell these places. You never knew a fieldstone fireplace was part of your needs—but now you have to have it. That's the big problem with catalogs.

A secondary problem is that often by the time you get the catalog, thumb through it, see a little gem, fall in love with it, consider buying it, and finally go to the local office to see it, the place has been sold.

And last but not least, another problem. A picture is

indeed worth a thousand words, but a camera can be terribly kind. And a real estate agent writing copy can do wonders for a place. Buying a place sight unseen is very dangerous. Avoid it.

If you can control and discipline yourself, however, there are practical reasons to send for a catalog or two. First, you can see some pictures of different parts of the country and learn something about the availability and beauty of land in different states. If you didn't know, for instance, that Wisconsin is as flat as a floor, maybe you'll notice that fact when you're looking at pictures. Or if you didn't know that Wisconsin gets pretty rolling in the northern part of the state, you might find that out too.

Catalogs have another good feature: they give you some idea of prices. You can do some comparison shopping from state to state by figuring out the cost per acre of like items, compare farm to farm, farm with pond to farm with pond, riverside to riverside, whatever. Don't think though that the catalog prices are necessarily representative of all the prices in the area; many places will be less expensive than the place in the catalog, but you will be able to make relative comparisons, like whether a farm with a pond costs less in Virginia or Vermont.

If you are a beginning looker, I recommend catalogs to you. They're informative, fun, and slightly addictive. However, the information you're going to get will be general; the fun you're going to have is nothing compared to actually looking for and having a piece of land; and as for the addictive part, you run the risk of falling in love with a piece of property that's already been sold.

Order a catalog from:

> Strout Realty
> Box 2757
> Springfield, Missouri 65803

United Farm Agency
612 West 47th
Kansas City, Missouri 64112

RECREATION DEVELOPMENT LAND

Some pages back I went into a short condemnation of recreation development land. I said that it is relatively expensive land compared to other property in the area. And I mentioned the possibility of it being less private and at the same time more highly taxed than other places in the same community.

Development land cannot be dismissed so briefly. It may fit your needs, and there's an awful lot of it for sale these days. With the help of HUD's Office of Interstate Land Sales, I've gathered this information on the subject.

If you've heard stories of how people were cheated on development property, there's some truth to it. People have been cheated, but they could have avoided it. What I'm getting at is that it is going to be up to you and your lawyer to make sure that the development land you buy is everything you expect it to be. Don't rely on the claims that nice smiling salesman gives you. He's selling for a commission, not necessarily accurately or truthfully.

Before you sign anything, ask the salesman for the property report. This is a document which is filed with HUD's Office of Interstate Land Sales. It consists of around fifty questions which the developer must answer. The questions touch on things like whether there are any liens currently on the property; the water and sewage availability, along with other services and utilities, and whether you will have to pay a maintenance charge for them. Also there's a list

find north
with the help of the big
dipper. The two stars in
the cup point the way to
the nearest bright star, Polaris.
It's north.

of the recreational facilities, with details on when they will be completed, and whether you will be expected to help pay for them above and beyond the sale price of the land. Plus a host of other rather technical bits like zoning ordinances and your risks should the development fail or go into bankruptcy.

The property report looks pretty official. It will impress you with its details and maybe overwhelm you with its legal language. Please take it to a lawyer and go over it carefully together. You will then know what the developer is really offering you—at least, in writing.

Which brings me to another point. At the beginning of this property report, HUD makes a big disclaimer that HUD is not endorsing or recommending this land necessarily and that furthermore, HUD has not inspected the property or dug into the accuracy of the details on the report.

Then why make the report, you might ask. Well, if the report is made, the promises are made in writing, and if the developer later fails to deliver what he said he would, The Office of Interstate Land Sales thinks you may be able to sue the developer.

One other thing about the property report. You have the right to cancel a contract you've signed if you were not given the property report before you signed. Also, if you weren't given the report forty-eight hours before signing the contract, you can cancel the contract—unless you signed a contract that had a small type clause in which you waived this right.

Once you've looked at the property report with a lawyer, the other big thing to do is take a close look at the land itself. Compare what you see to what you read. Then ask the salesman for the contract, and take it and the property report to your lawyer once more.

You may in fact be about to sign a contract which has a clause in it that reads: "no representations, oral or written, are relied upon which are not set forth in this agreement." That means that all the goodies you were promised by the salesman and even the property report are now sort of out the window. The contract is the thing that says what's really going to happen. So your understanding of the contract is vital.

If everything looks fair and square, go ahead, buy.

FARM MAGAZINES

Each cover is a treat. On one is a foggy close-up of apple trees in blossom, another shows a hind view of a dairy cow who has won prizes for her udder, another is a spilling bag of beans. They're all beautiful, and inside is still another way to find some land in the country.

Whether the magazine is published nationally or regionally, in the back are the want ads. You may get some really good leads here. The farms listed in these ads run from big operations complete with the seller's equipment and stock to small pieces of bare land. The ads are put in the magazines by real estate agents and individuals, and include telephone numbers or mailing addresses if you're interested, or an assigned number to refer to when you inquire of the classified department of the magazine.

Naturally, in the small space of a want ad, the seller really zaps the high spots and selling points of his farm. If the ad really leans on the berry business, or the barn equipment, you know that's the best feature of the farm and you'll pay extra for the advantage of continuing that particular business in the seller's footsteps. So if you're

not going in for berries or a forty-head dairy thing complete
with manure spreader, go right on past these ads. Keep
looking down the column for the one ad that sounds a little
bell in your brain. You'll see one, I promise.

Here are some samples of things taken from one
magazine that did things to me.

> 80 acres timber land. Norway pine, white
> pine, white birch. Good hunting area.
> $4000
>
> 40 acres, small stream. 2 bedroom home
> with garage. $6000
>
> 40 acres. Furnished 8 x 26 trailer. $3500
>
> 80 acres at the "top" of the Green Hills.
> Beautifully wooded, joins 40,000 acres of
> forest, cropland. Panoramic view. $11,500
>
> 160 acres. 30 acre lake $15,000

Besides the images these particular ads conjure up, a
nice thing about them is that there's a price given. Occasionally want ads tweak you with some orgiastic description
and when you get to the end, there's no price, just an
address. It's been our experience that these ads are for
pretty expensive land. After writing up all that wonder-
fulness, it just didn't make sense to tell people the land
costs an arm and a leg. The seller hopes that by tickling
your interest he can get you out there in person, have you
fall in love with the place, and hang the expense. If you're
on an economy trip, investigate a couple of the priceless
things and see if you agree; if so, don't follow up on ads
with no price listed from then on.

Mother Earth News is a fantastic magazine. It comes out bi-monthly and is full of ecology articles, suggestions for simpler living, and a section called "Positions and Situations" where you can get some leads on land for sale.

THE MOTHER EARTH NEWS

PO Box 38
Madison, Ohio 44057

If you know the state you want to settle in, there's undoubtedly a farm magazine or two that deal with the agriculture of the area. Find out which magazine it is, and buy a few copies. Not only will you get some great want ads; you'll also get an idea of the variety of land uses throughout the state, how the timber prices are going, what to feed a horse to keep him healthy, where to get free mulches, or how to sell your own produce. If you want good recipes, farm nostalgia, first aid tips, or anything else that applies to living and growing, you'll probably find it in a farm magazine sooner or later.

Besides advice on farm living, there's another treat in farm magazines: the help wanted section. Yes, it's a lousy section in city newspapers, where all they seem to want today is a typist or a security guard, but in farm magazines the help wanted section can start you wondering. Lots of these little ads are looking for a "sober" young man to help with chores or do certain jobs on the farm. Whatever the job is, it usually includes a house or at least living quarters. If you're not exactly flush with cash to spend on your own farm and you happen to be male, you could try getting one of these jobs, get a salary, lots of experience, maybe even a house and enough land for a garden.

RODALE'S TWO MILLIONTH ASSIST

Everything from rose hips to chicken shit has been written about by the Rodale people and their friends in a magazine called *Organic Gardening and Farming*. It's a magazine that I consider the treat of the century. *Organic Gardening* comes out monthly, and even Helen Nearing, one of the most articulate and true homesteaders in the whole wide world, writes them old-buddy-type letters, and they don't make a big deal of it, they just print it along with all the other letters to the editor.

Recently, *OGF* has added a new feature to the already jam-packed magazine: the Farm Market. All the farms listed here are for sale and all are organic farms according to the sellers. If you are especially anxious to find some land that hasn't been dusted and sprayed with chemicals, you're going to have a hard time finding it unless you get this magazine; it's the only place I know of where you can find a fairly reliable list of organic farms for sale. The acreage tends to be small in these listings; some of the places have houses, some don't; some have established organic orchards; some are in the mountains, some in the woods; many are expensive, others are cheap. Most are in this country, a few in Canada.

The Farm Market is only the beginning of helps the gardner or small-scale farmer can get from *OGF*. Read a few issues. It's a useful, delightful, honest, and fascinating magazine written almost completely by the folks who really know and practice organic earth methods. And it does an unequaled job of saying thank you to the sun, rain, moon, stars, and Mother Nature.

Thank you Mr. Rodale.

LOCAL NEWSPAPERS

Fantastic sources. Once you've narrowed your land search to a county or a town area, the local paper's advertisements can really help you find what you're after.

Want ads are placed by farmers who want to sell the land themselves rather than go through a real estate agent, and you may find your place the same way—without an agent. Just check the want ads. There are plenty of them

Local papers are full of good reading and good ads.

in the paper, sometimes all through the whole eight pages of it. But don't think that a want-ad farm is necessarily cheaper. I have to say it: it ain't necessarily so. These days farmers are often as aware of prices as the agents are, and they're perfectly willing to put a big tag on their farm. Farmers talk to each other, and when anything is sold in their area it's a safe assumption that every single one of them knows the price it went for, right down to the cents. And, too, every man thinks his farm is nicer than that mudhole that sold. So, while he's composing his want ad at the kitchen table, he's going to put a nice price on his farm. Why not? Maybe he could call it a recreational farm and double, triple, or quadruple the price.

Now that I've gotten that off my chest, there is one obvious reason why these local want ads are helpful to you the land-hunter looking for a nice farm. All these want ads are selling land in the area you like best. Their market is limited pretty much to the community served by the paper, and outside, citified hoopla is at a premium. Also, it's likely that your toughest competition, the city slicker with lots of money, won't bother with this; he'll probably go straight to a realtor.

Along with the want ads in the back of the paper is another kind of ad. Yes, the realty people. They often buy a full-page ad and cram it full of property after property. These agents are getting pretty good at copywriting too; the word "rustic" keeps cropping up. (If you're looking for bargains, when an agent calls it rustic, it's expensive rustic.) "Trout stream" has come to replace "creek" in realty vocabulary, and "farmette" or "recreational farm" means one for city people, the dummies who want to putter and pay extra. In spite of these bits of jargon, however, the realty ads can give you a pretty complete listing of the places for sale in the area, while the want ads will give you the rest.

And there's more in local papers. There are auction notices and ads for back-tax land for sale. I'll tell you about each of these little tickets later, but for now take my word for it: they are still other ways to locate that land you want.

If you are not in town during the week to buy the local paper, subscribe to it. It's got ads and country sales; it's got "this and that" columns and social bits on who had a baby next to a column about someone who grew a thirty-pound potato. It's a delight. And it costs only ten cents for one paper per week, or about three dollars for a year's subscription. It's a buy, and it's worth every penny if you find your place through it.

In most rural communities there is usually another paper which carries nothing but advertisements and is delivered free to all homes in the area. Inquire about this cooperative advertising paper and then pay the postage to have it mailed to your home. It is usually the best source for real estate ads.

THE SECRET OF ZERO PER CENT SUCCESS

After all this talk about want ads, it may have occurred to you to put your own want ad in a local paper. Maybe you think you can find a seller this way. I can tell you that your efforts will produce no reasonable response. City people putting want ads for land in a local paper receive either outlandish answers or silence. And the readers get some good yuks at your expense.

COUNTRY AUCTIONS

The auction posters look like they've been dipped in three-month-old Easter egg dye. Ah, the watery blues, the 2 A.M. greens, the pee yellows. See one auction notice and you'll never miss the rest: they look like something that stepped out of 1880 with their hairy type and old drawings of cows. You'll like looking at them, and a good deal of the time they'll bring you good news.

Auction companies in the country make a poster up about a month before each auction and stick it up in stores, on telephone poles, and in the windows of their office, and at the same time they start putting little ads in the local paper. Look for these notices; they'll often tell you there's a farm up for sale, along with its furniture, machinery, and useful odds and ends. Each item is auctioned individually, and by looking at the poster you can see a complete list of everything for sale plus all the other information you'll need to know before you go. If you're looking for a farm, watch for the auctions, especially in the fall and spring. Those are the best seasons for farmers to quit; their work is either just over, or not started yet.

There's one thing you should do before you go to the country auction with the idea of buying the land and the house. Check the notice of sale and see what percentage of your bid is required as a good-faith payment. It varies between 5 and 15 per cent. This means if you win the bidding on the house and land with $8500 for instance, you should have in your pocket or in the bank somewhere between $425 and $1275, which you'll give on the auction spot to show you really intend to buy. Know how much cash you can put down as a good-faith payment and plan to bid accordingly.

On the day of the auction, which is usually Saturday or Sunday, put on your dress-up jeans and drive over. If the auction is supposed to start at twelve noon, it might not be till four or later before they get to auctioning off the house. That always comes last; after the plates, old chairs, tables, beds, manure spreaders, whatever. (If you're interested in beds—a safe assumption—you can pick one up at an auction for as little as one dollar or as much as $650.) While the furniture and things are being sold, you have time to look at the land, poke around the house, see how you like everything, and do your arithmetic.

When it comes time to auction off the house, try not to get nervous. Get toward the front of the crowd and hold hands with your friend so you don't trip or anything. You may find fifteen other people working toward the front too, but this kind of competition is pretty rare. As a matter of fact, you may be standing there all alone while the auctioneer tries to keep the crowd from wandering off into the twilight, and looks at you out of the corner of his eye. Relax. Here's what will happen and what to do.

The auctioneer will announce the terms of the sale: percentage required to hold your bid, how much land is involved, and related official stuff. He'll usually say that the owner reserves the right to reject any bid. You listen.

The auctioneer and his assistant (the man with the pad of paper in his hand and the auction service's name embroidered on the back of his shirt, the one whose job it is to scan the crowd, keep track of bidders, and add syncopation to the auction chant) start the song. Running it all together, faster and faster, pretty soon it sounds like yaba yaba yeeeaaaba ba. The gist of the tune will come across, though, and it'll be something like, "Here's a dandy little place, dandy farm, who'll give me two thousand? Who'll give me two? Do I hear two thousand?" Don't. Anyone can start the bidding anywhere he wants. The auctioneer's just trying to start high. The lower the starting bid, the longer it takes to get high . . . and that's to your advantage. You can stand there and wait for someone else to open, or you can raise your hand a little if you're surrounded and say, "Five hundred." He'll see you.

"Whoop," goes the assistant.

"Whee, I got five hundred. Five hundred's the bid. Do I hear a thousand? One thousand dollars. Do I hear one?" says the auctioneer. "Yep! Whoop!" sings the assistant, meaning there's someone in the crowd who's bidding against you. Relax. You don't have to move fast. The auctioneer will keep up the patter while you think. As soon as you know someone's bidding against you, too, the really pro thing is to keep your face void of expression; don't turn and scan the crowd with your squinty eyes. Don't try to find out who the cat is that's giving you a stomachache. Relax.

The auctioneer knows where you are and hasn't forgotten you. He'll turn to you as soon as that other bidder shuts up and say, "Wehhh, I've got one. One thousand. Thousand's the bid. Do I hear two? Two? Two?" Okay. There are two things you can do. You can say fifteen hundred if you want; you don't have to bid what the auctioneer suggests. He just works there, he's just keeping the bidding moving. So you can say fifteen hundred, or, if you know it's going to go a lot higher than two thousand, you can say yes, you'll bid two, and you can do it with a blink of your eyes. You can say yes by just nodding your head, smiling, sticking out your tongue, anything. And he'll know you've raised the bid to two thousand. Sometimes at an auction, especially when people get into this blinking thing, it's impossible to tell who's bidding. All the little yesses are invisible to everyone except the auctioneer. People think it's cool to silently up the bid. Try it; you'll look as if you know what you're doing.

Now it's the other guy's turn. Or maybe a new bidder gets into the act about now. Whatever, after a chorus of whoops, wees, bayaeeahs, and blinks, the auctioneer always checking back with those still in the bidding, someone will win. If you don't want to be the winner, if it's getting to the money level you can't handle, all you do when it comes your turn to bid is shake your head no or turn away out of the circle and the auctioneer will count you out. He won't look back at you again, unless you change your mind and get your hand in the air again.

What happens if you win the bidding? Laugh. Hug. Get rid of the tension. And as soon as he's done saying hello to his friends in the crowd, the auctioneer will come over with his little pad and pen and get your name and your check. Of course, he'll act businesslike until he gets all the things he needs to take to the owner when he gives him your offer; then he'll get loose. "Nice place, that's for sure," he'll say. "Hope you young folks enjoy it. We can use some young blood around here. Why, I gotta boy, he's eighteen now, plays ball and can't wait to get out of this town. Now, I sure wish he'd . . ." and so on, just like the rest of the gabby good people you meet so often in the country.

If the owner thinks your bid is high enough, you've got the place. If not, he'll make a counteroffer and you can go through the shenanigans if you've got the inclination and the money to do it. If not, you get your check back and you haven't lost a thing. And you're really ready, this time, for the next auction.

CHEAP THRILLS

Hear the word "free" and you get excited. It never fails. Oh wooooooow, land's just there for the taking . . . for the living. Fantastic. All I gotta do is get *to* it. And I'll live so natural, I'll live so free. I'm gonna live off the government land . . . and the land's for free! Where is it? you say, grabbing your Swiss Army knife.

A good question. Let me sound like a grown-up for a minute and say that free land just doesn't exist.

Free land is most often associated with homesteading. And when the Homesteading Act was made up it was 1862. Before the Civil War. There was real territory then. There weren't 220 million people scrounging around for a piece of the action. In 1862, there was plenty of land to go around and there weren't airplanes, cars, mobile homes, TV dinners, cities, and suburbs. Now we've got cities and suburbs and things are getting tight, what with schools, roads, wars, and a hundred other things. Nobody's about to give something to you. They could sell that so-called homesteading land for a pile of dough. And that's just what they do. May I suggest that you forget government free land entirely? The Homesteading Act went out with the do-si-do.

BUYING BACK-TAX LAND

When someone doesn't pay his local taxes, his local

friends and neighbors, thoughtfully represented by the city or town, will wonder why. The town keeps rather thorough records on these matters. And when it gets pale and wan from lack of funds, the town will try to locate the person who's holding out on them. When they find out who it is, maybe it's a nasty-letter routine for a while, but pretty soon it gets official and legal, and if the owner can't or won't pay the local taxes, the town claims the land he owns for taxes due. He's hustled off. Then they put the place up for sale to recoup their lost money.

This is a sad thing and, luckily for most landowners, it's pretty rare, but it occasionally happens; so if you're looking for bargain land it's something to know about.

Tax sales, if they happen, happen once a year. The sale is announced with notices in the local newspapers, and when you see one you should go to the county tax assessor's office in the county seat to find out particulars. The tax assessor will have information on where the farm is, how much land is involved, and other technicalities of the sale, which vary from state to state. The notice in the newspaper is easy to miss, by the way, so if you're really interested in this method of land-buying it makes sense to check in with the tax assessor periodically.

Back-tax land is sold at auction and the highest bidder wins as long as the bid equals or surpasses the amount of taxes due. This minimum might be $100 or $1000 or more, depending on the farm. If you buy the farm, you also have to pay the cost of advertising the sale, which is, again, probably a small amount.

If you can find a back-tax auction it's likely you will pay a lot—lot less for the place than if the owner were selling it. He'd be interested in the real value of the place, while the state in this case just wants its tax money. However, if the seized land is currently mortgaged, you will probably be bidding against the bank that holds the mortgage, so, how big a bargain it is depends on who else is at the auction—and how much he wants the place.

There are several downers about buying a place for back taxes. First of all, you're not going to have a quick simple job in locating a place that suits you this way. If you're anxious to buy land, don't limit your search to the county tax assessor's office—you could have a very long wait. The second problem is knowing what you're getting into in terms of the state's laws. Before you buy, you should know the answers to two questions: Is the tax sale final in that state, or is there a period of redemption when the delinquent "owner" can return, repay you the tax money, cover court costs, and reclaim the land? Second, if there is a period of redemption, and you want to take the chance anyway of losing the place, does the state require that the prodigal owner also pay you for any improvements you made on the land? You may have built a house, for instance, during the grace period. Does he have to reimburse you for that before he can legally reclaim the place? These technicalities will affect your plans for the land and you should get the law clear in your mind before you buy. Ask the tax man, ask a lawyer, but definitely go into the auction knowing.

PEOPLE TO SEE

I've never seen a town that didn't have a hardware store. And if you get nutsy in hardware stores, you ought to meet the people who run the local one. They are often among the most prosperous people in town and are invariably helpful. The hardware store man always seems to know where the best fishing is, what to do about black hornets, how to attract birds, how to fix a spring house, and who's selling his farm. If you've got a question, ask the hardware store man. He's in constant contact with the farmers, because, like everywhere else these days, little things are always breaking down and the farmer has to fix it himself. He doesn't take it to some fancy shop and wait a month and a half for them to change the wrong tube. He goes to the hardware store, disgusted with another broken tool, tells his tale of woe to some sympathetic ears, buys five dollars' worth of gadgets, puts his money on the counter with one hand, hits the counter with the other, and shouts, "Someday, Larry, I'm gonna get out of this business! Sell my farm and get out!"

Go ahead. Ask the hardware store man where there's a farm for sale. You may hear of a couple. And if you don't have any luck the first time you stop there, go back again. Maybe on your second trip Larry will shout across the shovels as you come in the door, "Hi, John, good t' see you again." He remembers your name! "Say, you know that piece of land you wanted? Well, I was talkin' to Floyd Jones the other day and his wife wants to move to Florida. Thinks he might be going to sell out. Might stop out and see him." Do.

"Fill 'er up, check the oil, and do you know where there's any farms for sale?"

Everywhere you go. Ask your question. The wonderful thing about small towns is that people are not usually hesitant to talk. They will tell you what their town is like, how many times it rained last year, and who their neighbors are, and if they know someone is going to be moving away, they'll tell you that too. Even if it's a hunch. The one catch is that they'll want to know who you are too, so you'd better get rid of your city paranoia right away. Tell them your names, where you live, and talk about your childhood, your hobbies, your favorite wrench, anything that's approppriate and friendly.

Ask a few questions in the country. Make a few friends. Maybe find a country place.

3

PAYING

Money's not the most important thing in life—but if it's a problem, it's a big problem. And it's true that finding the money to set yourself a few miles away from the city may be a lot more difficult than deciding you want out of the city in the first place.

There are many places and people in the business of loaning money, and they all have their particular ways, demands, and complexities. But the one thing that underlies all their procedures and determines whether or not you get the money from any of them is you. How much money do you have? Do you have any money making knowledge or skill? Do you have a good financial record? Before the banks and real estate agents start asking you these questions, ask them of yourself. Know how much you can spend, make a reasonable estimate of your future income, and select a piece of land or a farm or a house on that basis. If you can't afford to buy a $30,000 farm, don't look at $30,000 farms. If you can afford to buy a $5000 farm, that's what you look for. It's a simple rule to have from the outset and it will save you some difficulty in the end. Know what you can spend before you start looking.

If you don't like the idea of paying money to get money,

Birches start a forest. Hardwood trees come later in the forest's life.

The paper bark on birches develops when the tree is about three years old.

then you will have to save and save and delay gratification until you have the total sale price in your pocket. This way you don't have to talk to bankers, you don't have to meet monthly payments, and you don't have to worry if you have a penniless year or someone gets sick. You buy the land outright.

But if you have to borrow, here are some general things about the attitudes of lenders just about everywhere.

1. The big-city bank where you deposit your city paycheck will probably not be interested in loaning you money to buy a place outside the "territory." Even if you are a good solid customer, they'll tell you they prefer to invest their money in their community so that they can reap future benefits from their involvement. This may be true to a degree; however, the main reason a bank won't loan you money to buy property far away is that they have no way of knowing the value of that property. This "territorial imperative" applies to every other lender as well. No one gives money unless he knows that money's going to buy something he considers fairly priced.

2. If you are female, you're in trouble. If you want to buy a piece of land all by yourself, even if you have a very, very good income by male society's standards, your income is always jeopardized by your baby potential, and you will have a hard time getting a loan. The lender is male, don't forget, or at least represents an institution which is incredibly male-oriented; and as you sit there explaining your financial condition, he's undboutedly thinking that all this poor creature needs is a good man, not a piece of real estate. Furthermore, if you are female and married and the two of you want to buy a farm, the same thing applies. You, dear young lady, with your nice salary, your good business head, and your talent, generally don't matter

a whit. Your income is "temporary." Your function in life is procreation, right? And women don't work when they have families. So the lender's decision is often based solely on the husband's earnings: on *his* money, *his* financial position, *his* qualifications. You don't count. You just work there. This is unfair, but true.

3. Unimproved, bare land is hard to get a loan on. It's nearly impossible unless you have some collateral to leave with the man. Stock, bonds, real estate that you own, and the cash value of a life insurance policy are the most common types of collateral. Rarely do lenders give you dollar for dollar on these items; often they require collateral that exceeds the value of the loan, but just what the percentage is varies with the situation.

4. When you get a loan, most lenders will require that you insure the place against fire and natural disasters. If you want to borrow money, you should buy or agree to buy an insurance policy that will replace any building you have on the place. The lender sees buildings as added value to the land, and if they're gone the land is considered less valuable. If your barn burns down, you will have insurance to cover part of the cost at least of rebuilding and the land resumes its original value to the lender, the value he lent you money on, at the very least.

5. The big neon-lit generalization about lenders is that they have an exuberant respect for your money. The more you have, the more they wiggle their fingers and nod their heads.

6. One thing occurs to me about banks in particular. I'd say it's easier to get a loan from a bank that's located in a prosperous town. In the first place, they may have more depositors and, consequently, more money to loan out. In the second place, the economic health and spirit

of the town are often a reflection of the individual banker himself. If he's oriented toward building up a nice, strong community, he'll take more "risks" with borrowers who have good ideas. He'll give store owners the money to expand, improve, or remodel. He'll make loans to the person who wants to start a little store with his hand-made furniture. If, on the other hand, the banker is oriented more toward protecting the bank and the status quo, he'll be very careful to loan money only to sure things. His son, for instance.

BANKS AND SAVINGS AND LOANS

If you go to a bank or a savings and loan to get money for your new house and land, you're talking about a mortgage. A mortgage is an agreement between you and the bank that they'll give you a certain amount of money, and in exchange you'll give them a lien on the thing you buy. This lien means that, should you be unable to keep up your monthly payments, the bank can step in, foreclose on the mortgage, and sell your land. The proceeds of the foreclosure sale are kept as payment of your debt, and any money in excess of what you owed is given to you. And you're out. Foreclosure is a big pain to the bank (this hurts me more than it does you) and they really don't like to do it. It's paperwork, dunning letters, legal activities, and sometimes a money-losing proposition for them—so that's why they're so careful about whom they lend money to in the first place.

To assure themselves that this nasty procedure is unlikely with you, they require you to give them a statement of financial condition when you apply for a loan. Everything you own is listed in detail on this statement and every debt as well. You include credit references, employment history, and a host of personal facts. A lawyer can help you draw this up if you want, but be sure everything is accurate either way, because the bank or savings and loan checks it all out—carefully.

Banks are especially interested in how much cash you have, how much you are likely to have from whatever work you do, and how you have behaved when you borrowed money before. If some bank foreclosed on you a while ago and now you're applying for another mortgage, forget it. However, if you have a very good reason why you didn't make it that time, tell the lender every nook and cranny of the former situation. It may help. And if there was some computer mix-up about a three-dollar purchase with a big company once upon a time, and you know that your credit rating is messed up because of it, give that a thorough explanation too.

By the way, it is your legal right to see and, if necessary, correct your credit record.

INTEREST

The interest rate on your loan will vary depending on the bank you go to and the general state of money in the country. If money is tight all over and the bank is cautious, the interest rate will be high. If money is available all over and the bank is a sort of risk-taking gunslinger who wants to make a lot of mortgages, the interest rate will be low. You should investigate what each bank or loaner in your area is charging for loans because you may find one is charging 7 per cent while another is charging 7½ per cent.

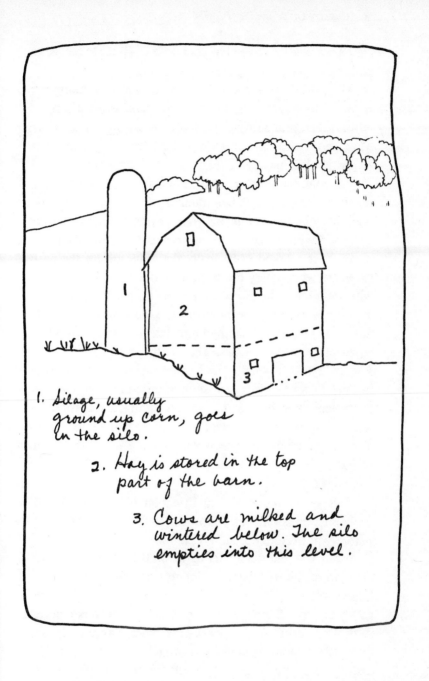

1. Silage, usually ground up corn, goes in the silo.

2. Hay is stored in the top part of the barn.

3. Cows are milked and wintered below. The silo empties into this level.

Half a per cent on the end of your nose is a lot. Do business with the 7 per center if they'll have you.

The total interest you pay will be greater if the mortgage is over a long term, say twenty-five years, while a shorter term, fifteen-year mortgate will cost you less in total interest. Most people realize that over a short term they will have larger monthly payments than over the long term.

The long term mortgage is more advantageous, according to some people. Their thinking goes something like this. If inflation continues, your payments in the future are made with cheaper and cheaper dollars. For instance, if you have worked in basically the same job for the past ten years, your salary has been increased just to keep pace with inflation. Therefore, you have a greater number of dollars today. But, the number of dollars you owe on a mortgage made ten years ago remains the same (minus the payments you have made). The mortgage payment, therefore, will take a smaller and smaller percentage of your income as time goes on, assuming inflation continues. If the reverse happens, and deflation during a recession or depression occurs, the exact opposite would be the case. The longer term mortgate would be a disadvantage. You would be paying a greater percentage of your decreasing income as time went on.

This is obviously a simplification of a complicated economic situation, but you ought to consider these facts before you make a decision on a mortgage.

When you and the lender agree on the interest rate and the term of the mortgate, the interest rate will not change. You won't get a letter five years from now saying you're going to pay 10 per cent interest instead of 7 per cent. A deal's a deal. And it works the other way too. If, in the future, money is being lent at an interest rate smaller than the one you bargained for, like 5 per cent, you keep right on paying that 7 per cent. A deal's a deal, on that mortgage at least.

One other thing. You don't pay taxes on money spent for interest on a loan. Interest is deductible. In the early years of a mortgage your interest payments are heaviest, therefore you may find that the first few years on the farm payment are almost all deductible.

THE DOWN PAYMENT

If you want to buy a place that costs $10,000, the bank won't lend you the whole amount. They want you to have some vested interest in this deal so you won't say, "Oh, heck, I've tried this for three weeks now, I don't like it, I'm just gonna let the bank have this turkey back. I'm going to Australia." To make sure that you won't go to Australia, the bank requires a down payment to help ensure your continued commitment. Just how much the down payment is depends on the bank. Some banks want you to have a down payment of 20 per cent of the purchase price before they give you the loan. That would be $2000 cash for a $10,000 farm, and then the bank would loan you $8000 or 80 per cent. Other banks however, may want you really committed with a 30 to 40 per cent cash down payment; then they don't have to give you so much. Check and see what different banks in your area require, and of course check to see you've still got sufficient cash for the down payment.

CLOSING COSTS

While you're counting your money and figuring what

you can put down, allocate part of your cash for closing costs. These are the various fees and expenses that come due on the day you take title to the property, the first day of your mortgage. You may have to pay to have the courthouse record the title change, you may have to pay a lawyer his due, you may have to pay the seller for any taxes he paid that extend into your period of ownership and you may have incurred other costs if you had the land surveyed or if you've bought title insurance. The total closing costs will vary, depending on you and the situation, but as you're going through the process of buying, keep a running total of these expenses so you'll have the cash when the time comes.

RIGHT OF PREPAYMENT

Once you and the banker agree on the terms, interest rate and so on, there's one other thing you should discuss with him, or any other lender, for that matter: the right of prepayment. That is, paying off the loan before it's gone full term.

Let's say you have a mortgate with a bank when you suddenly find $50,000 buried in a paper sack in your garden. You decide to pay off your twenty-five-year mortgate ten ycars early. What happens? First of all, you'll want to pay just the remaining principal of the loan. (If you borrowed $10,000 and have so far paid them $5000 on the principal plus a lot of interest as well, you'll want to pay the bank just the remaining principal, or $5000.) Now naturally, the bank is not going to be too hot for this idea because they make money from the interest on the loan, and if you prepay just the outstanding principal, they are losing all that interest they would have gotten if your loan had gone full term. So. The right of prepayment, with a bank at least, invariably

A good used truck
is hard to find; the
owners drive them till
they drop. For a cheap
good truck, go to the
big city used car lots
that sell the cast-off
Park District trucks. Very
few miles, good brakes,
and well maintained.

includes a penalty. Sometimes it's three months' interest, sometimes it's 3 per cent of the total interest, sometimes it's an arm and a leg—it depends on the bank. Find out what the story is when you apply for a loan.

This problem of prepayment arises at other times too. Like if you decide to sell the farm before you've paid off the mortgage; if you want to sell off part of the farm while the mortgage is still in effect; or if you want to refinance the mortgage during a time when the bank is charging much less interest for their mortgages than you are currently paying on an "old" mortgage. All these situations are complicated if you do not have the right of prepayment. Get acquainted with your bank's particular ways of handling these situations and see how you like them. In particular, see how you like their penalties when you prepay.

MORTGAGING THE COMMUNE

You and your friends have to do all the things an individual has to do in order to get a mortgage. Statements of financial condition and the rest of it have to be filed by every participating male. (The communal woman has no financial worth as far as the banker is concerned, remember. She's just living with all those men.) Before you assume the bank or lender is going to throw you out without giving you a chance, here's a fact. The lender likes to see responsibility spread around. They like to see three men accountable for the loan instead of one. It's a safer thing for them. If one guy stubs his toe, there are two others there to pick him up.

While you all are talking to the banker or whoever, psych him out a little. Try to look like he does. Try to use words that he uses, like cooperative, instead of commune. Make every effort to appear stable in his eyes, he'll trust you more. When you have to get a loan to buy your freedom, these little concessions are insignificant.

ALTERNATIVES

There are other places in the financial world besides banks, and savings and loan institutions. And if you don't like banks or banks don't like you it doesn't mean you'll be stuck in the city for the rest of your life. Here are some alternatives.

INSURANCE COMPANY AND
FARM MORTGAGE COMPANIES

If the banker hasn't bounced you on his knee and called you son, or sir, and he refuses to loan you money, ask him to tell you about insurance company loans and farm mortgage companies. The banker has these companies' requirements for loans and you may fit them. The banker can make the loan for you.

TAKE ON THE PRESENT OWNER'S MORTGAGE

This little move can't be done without the bank knowing about it . . . so if the bank's the problem, this won't be the solution. But if the bank's happy and you're happy, take on the present owner's mortgage, revise the terms of the loan (the interest rate probably), release the present owner legally from any responsibility to you or the bank, and go on your merry landowning, installment-paying way.

FARMERS HOME

The Farmers Home Administration has three familiar initials for the city person, and your first reaction may be, "Oh, yeah, FHA. That's the one that guarantees loans that banks make." Wrong. Farmers Home Administration is not *that* FHA. That FHA is the Federal Housing Administration, and they only fool around in city property.

Farmers Home, as they are affectionately called in the country, deals only in rural property. If the local banker hasn't greeted you with open arms and checkbooks, go on over to Farmers Home. Your rejection is their first criterion. They make loans to people the banks refuse.

Generally, the loans are made at 5 per cent interest over a period of 40 years to full or part time farmers. And the way in which you repay the loan is often tailored to coincide with the time your income is coming in.

To get a loan you apply to your county Farmers Home office and they'll supply you with the right forms for your type of loan. They'll smile nicely at you and treat you more casually, and you'll feel different than you did at the bank. That's not to say that Farmers Home is definitely going to give you this loan; it's just that they'll be pretty damn nice, even if they turn you down. But more about that later.

If you can't find the office than handles loans in your area, write to the Farmers Home Administration, Department of Agriculture, Washington, D.C. 20250, and they'll tell you the nearest place for you. Then go over and get your smiles and forms.

You will be asked on these forms to answer pretty much the same questions the bank asked you. Like how much money you have, where you got it, how much you will have in the future. After you've filled this out, they run a little credit check on you. You fill out still another form and hand the whole shot over to their county committee. The county committee is usually made up of three well-informed farmers from the area who pass judgment on your application. Most likely you will not be invited to this meeting concerning your hopes, dreams, aspirations, good intentions, and high character. But you can ask to come; all they can do is turn you down. If the committee feels you are a wonderful individual, it will then set out to appraise the land you want to buy. It will set a figure and will loan you only that much. If the seller wants more than Farmers Home will give, you persuade him differently or else make up the difference yourself.

Once the loan is made, the interest rate and particulars won't change. You can continue to pay the presently teeny interest rate and principal from now until you own the place. But don't make too much money while you're living out there, because Farmers Home will be back in touch with you maybe five years from now with a little form to fill out. Well, well, the same form you filled out awhile ago; How much ya got? How much ya gonna have? and so on. If it turns out that you are doing so well that a local banker would now consent to do business, that's what you have to do—refinance the loan with the bank. You're doing too well for Farmers Home.

Back to you. To get a loan from Farmers Home you have to be, as I said, an undesirable to the local loaning establishment. If you are earning around $9000 or less right now, you probably got turned down at the bank, and you'll probably get a nice welcome at Farmers Home. To qualify for a loan, you have to show signs of good character and dependability. If you want to buy a piece of land, they

When it's cold outside, the
farmer wears 2 undershirts,
3 flannel shirts, 2 pairs of
pants, overalls, heavy socks,
and a warm coat. Layering
clothing is warmer than
one huge coat.

expect you to use it for some sort of agriculture, crops, animals, trees, fish, and so on. Since they have this expectation, they have a matching requirement that you have some farming experience or be currently working a farm. You're expected too, on your big new farm, to make most of your income from it and do most of the labor yourself.

Once you've gotten acquainted with the people in the Farmers Home office down the road, keep in touch, especially if you want to put in a pond sometime in the future or plant a forest, drill a well, put in a real john, set up a roadside stand, buy livestock, buy seeds, or do just about anything as long as it's related to shelter, operating a farm, or conserving the earth. It's pretty likely that Farmers Home will have some money for you. For a small price.

LAND BANK LOANS

Federal Land Bank Loans aren't as well known as the Farmer's Home, but they have a good supply of money for borrowers. The Land Bank was set up quite a while ago to give first mortgages to people who will earn their living by farming. And you can get help to buy or improve your farm through one of the 750-member associations. These associations are supervised by the government, as are all financial operations, but they don't get a penny from Uncle Sam. Their source of funds is from the sale of bonds to the public, and they call themselves "the largest fully farmer-owned cooperative credit system in the world."

Presently, the Land Bank is ready to loan up to 85 per cent of the appraised value of a farm at an interest rate of 7 per cent for as long as 40 years. The most interesting thing about the Land Bank as far as you're concerned, however, is that you don't have to have experience in farming to get a loan from them. You could, for instance, finance 40 acres with them, rent the land to someone as cropland or pasture, and hold a job in the city.

If you have a loan with a Land Bank, you are required to buy stock in the association equal to 5 per cent of your loan, and so become part of the big happy group. You're a part owner, and as such are entitled to dividends, a share of the earnings when the cooperative comes out ahead at the end of the year. These dividends will reduce your payments some.

If you want to try for a Land Bank Loan, go to the local Land Bank office—there's usually one for every two or three counties. Or if you don't know where it is, ask your county agricultural agent or write to the Farm Credit Administration, Washington, D.C. 20578.

LAND CONTRACTS

A land contract is so simple, it's a little confusing. And it's probably one of the most common methods of farm purchase used today. A land contract is a sales agreement between you and the seller; no banks and no other intermediaries are involved. It's just you and the seller. You pay him a down payment, often less than you would if you were getting a mortgage through a bank. You pay the seller the monthly installments, and they're often at a lower interest rate than the bank is currently charging. The seller, however, keeps title to the land until you've paid him in full.

A land contract is an excellent way to buy, especially if other finance places are lukewarm to you. Discuss this

with the seller and you may be able to buy his farm on
a contract. From his point of view, a land contract has
its advantages. If he sells you the farm for $15,000, and
you get a mortgage from the bank, the seller gets a couple
of checks totaling $15,000. Boom, like that. His problem
is that $15,000 may up his income so high for the year
that it will result in unusually high taxes. But if instead
you spread the payment out over several years, it saves
him money in tax payments. A land contract can be nice
for you, and nice for the seller. A Land Contract is a Good
Thing.

After that ballyhoo, here's a caution about land contracts.
You have to be careful about how the contract is worded,
and you may need a lawyer to advise you on the particular
contract and the state's laws. The important thing to find
out is what happens if you should miss a payment. State
law determines how these contracts read, and in some states,
land contracts give the seller (who retains legal title,
remember) the right to immediately foreclose if you miss
a payment. That means off—now. And no money, nothin'.
However, even where this procedure is state law, common
law has intervened to varying degrees to protect you.
Usually, the seller is required to take his foreclosure through
the courts, and that takes six to eight months—enough time,
hopefully, for you to make good your contract and continue
your payments. This is the stickler to land contracts, and
you'd be smart to know how the state law reads—and even
smarter to have a friendly chat with a good local attorney.
While you and the seller are talking things over, discuss
the right of prepayment without penalty. In my opinion
you should have this right, because this man will legally
hold title to the property until you have paid him in full.
Should you want to sell the farm before you've paid him

Party lines are
common in rural areas.
Calls are limited to 6
minutes apiece usually,
and when you've talked
enough there's a little
warning beep to remind
you.

off, you may have technical trouble selling the farm. If you do not have the right to pay him in advance you could end up in a lot of legal hassles and unpleasantness.

It's important in a land contract arrangement that you and the seller get along. He's not a banker that you'll probably never see again; he's likely to be a neighbor and a hale fellow in the community. Don't jeopardize your happiness by being unreasonable. If all you want is a fair deal, not too much or too little, you may get a new friend thrown into the bargain and some good words spoken on your behalf.

THINGS TO KNOW WHEN YOU PAY

When you buy land, there are a number of confusing words that crop up when you've just about finished the negotiating and are ready to settle the deal. They are all part of a very fancy and old vocabulary that evolved over years and years of buying and selling property in this country.

I'll give them to you along with some very basic definitions.

Title. Title and ownership are synonymous. Title is conveyed by the deed.

Deed. A piece of paper in which the seller conveys title to the property to the buyer.

Abstract. A literal history of all the owners of a certain piece of property. The abstract for your land will list the names of everyone who ever owned it, all the way back to the name of the original settler who bought the land from the government.

Any time land changes hands, any time title changes,

the abstract should be searched. This search is nothing more than checking the document to see that each person who sold the land in the past had the right to sell it. Searching the abstract will determine whether this current owner as well, has the right to sell the land to you.

When you are ready to sign on the dotted line, don't do it until you have a local lawyer search the abstract and assure you that everything is in order. You will pay the lawyer for his services, and they are worth every penny of the expense because if the abstract is not in order, does not clearly show that each former owner had the right to sell, you can be really clobbered in the future. If, for instance, the thirteenth owner, way back in 1878, didn't sell the land but gave it to a friend who didn't get title, that thirteenth owner's great-great-great-grandson can appear on the scene and start making claims to the land. In short, get a local lawyer to determine that this is an impossibility with your particular property.

Title Insurance. You are likely to have heard this term in the city. It is not a particularly common phrase in the country but it deserves explanation. Title insurance people basically do the same thing that your country lawyer does: they search the abstract and charge you for their services. And once they have assured themselves that the abstract is in order, they will agree to issue you title insurance. This insurance is a way that urban property holders have cushioned themselves against some unforeseen fluke. You can occasionally get title insurance in the country, but it is somewhat more difficult.

What's the fluke? Well, maybe the abstract was so complicated and intricate that when the insurance people checked it out they missed something. It's the great-

great-great-grandson of the thirteenth owner again, and he's ready to fight you in court for it. If you have title insurance, the title company will fight for you in court and pay the expenses. And if the worst happens, and he is proven to own the land, the title insurance people will usually reimburse you for the full amount you paid for the farm.

LAND SURVEYS

When the government began selling off plots to settlers, they broke great masses of land into measurements called sections, then marked the corners of sections by carving a tree and assigning a witness tree nearby in case the marker tree was destroyed. Next the section was broken into smaller pieces and sold. All this was fine years ago, but marker and witness trees are often gone now and exact boundaries of land have become vague. A farmer may assume that a wood lot is on his property because the man he bought it from said so. In truth, the wood lot may belong to a neighbor who doesn't realize it.

Many authorities and lenders say that your should have land surveyed or mapped before you buy it. A licensed surveyor is a person who computes the correct boundaries, and the cost of his survey is not cheap.

Having land surveyed before you buy it may cause some problems. The survey may take a few months and you and the owner may have no inclination to wait that long. Furthermore, a survey sometimes entails getting the neighbors to acquiesce to the surveyor's report. They may not be too keen on establishing new boundaries.

But if you want your money's worth, the cost and the

time involved in a land survey may not matter to you when you weigh it against the certain knowledge that you've bought the number of acres you've paid for—that what is said to be yours, is yours for sure.

FARM INSURANCE

While you're running around trying to get money to buy the farm, there's one other thing you should investigate: farm insurance. The only type you need right away is fire insurance on the barn, the house, and any other essential buildings. It's very expensive to replace something that's burned down, and in the country there aren't fifteen or twenty fire stations all staffed and ready to save you. Volunteer firemen are the rule in the country, and though they really do their utmost, it's often too late. You can't afford not to have fire coverage—unless, of course, everything's made of stone and asbestos.

The former owner's policy can sometimes be transferred to you when you take possession, or you can go to your own company. Either way, there are a couple of things that can raise or lower your particular premium. If you don't live on the farm full time, your premium will be higher than average. While you're away a fire could start and no one will be there to call the fire department. So you pay extra for your absence.

If you have a pond or a good-sized stream near your buildings, your premium will be lower. Fire hydrants are rare in the country, and with your pond, the firemen can just pull up and start pumping. So, if you are looking for

Pigs are as intelligent
as dogs and they often
figure out ways to
get around the fences
made to contain them.

further rationalizations for paying extra for land with water on it, this is one. The water will lower your insurance.

As for the other types of insurance—liability, health, life, and crop—you can decide whether they're necessary for you. A few dollars a year can save you some real trouble in the future, so you might consider them.

4

THE GIFTS AND TAKES OF OLD HOUSES

Right about now I ought to say that we have an old house, and that colors my objectivity a little. New homes are fantastic, especially the ones you've made yourself; but old houses are where I really live—it's just me. I try to cover up the romantic side of my personality with the rationale that buying an old house is a kind of recycling. You don't have to buy new wood, new glass, new anything in order to build your shelter. It's already built. You don't have to consume new materials; more trees, more nails, more cement, more this, more that. You just move into an old house, change it just enough, and spare trees and waste in the process.

Old houses are strong friends. Think about buying one. They're loyal and true and they're sorry when they leak or creak or make noise while you're trying to sleep. And they do their best to make up for these annoyances by giving you long porches with carved posts and flowers growing up them; with dark old wooden floor and tall doorways; with high rooms, strange attics, huge kitchens, and a habit for doing things the old way.

Besides the romance and the recycling aspect, old houses have many real advantages over buying bare land and then

building on it. Other people have lived there, so there will
be a supply of water available. Water, you know, doesn't
come through some incomprehensible, invisible pipe from
the city waterworks when you're in the country. When
you're in a rural area, you supply your own water, not
to mention a lot of other services that you take for granted
in the city—things like trash collections, snow plows,
shoveled sidewalks, sewage treatment, and several other
things. Your water, your sewage, your trash, your snow
are now your responsibilities. So if you buy an old farmhouse, it's a sure thing there's going to be some kind of
water supply—a well, a spring, or whatever—already there,
along with some kind of sewage accommodations. I'll tell
you how to judge the types you might run into a little
later. But, as for your trash, there are lots of things you
can do with country trash. You can use the old wire trash
burner the farmer probably has out back, or you can save
your newspapers and cardboard boxes, use them as mulch
in the garden, hold them down with stones and take them
up when the season's over, or let them rot into the ground.
Paper comes from trees, you know. The garbage goes in
the compost pile, naturally. And the cans—well, maybe
you can cut down on the cans you buy (you're going to
have a garden) and the cans you do buy make great little
planters for seedlings . . . and good protection for growing
gardens from insects and frost. Anyway, when you buy
an old farmhouse, it may come with a water supply, a
sewage system, and a trash can.

Another thing you are likely to get with an old house
is a road. It may sound simple-minded to say that a road
is a great advantage, but if you've been thinking of buying
bare land and then building an isolated house on it, part
of the job will be putting in a road, along with a septic

Basic compost pile.

Compost is quickly made by using shredded things like grass clippings. Run a lawn mower over weeds, straw or any material you want to throw in. You can put kitchen scraps in too. Then, turn the pile every 3 days. You should have 'dirt' in two weeks.

dirt
manure or bone meal
grass clippings
bare ground

tank or water supply, a well with pump, pipes, and a pressure tank. All quite expensive. It may cost you more for the land and necessities than it would to buy an existing place with all these things already done for you. If you buy bare land, as opposed to recycling an old house, the first thing you've got to do is put in a road.

If you want to put in a nice long road that'll give you lots of privacy, say a quarter of a mile long, it will cost you $1000 to $1500 just for the gravel and the hauling. This price does not include any clearing of timber you might have to do, it does not include any excavating you might have to do, and it does not include a final smooth grading of the surface of the road, or any later grading. It's a bare-bones estimate. The total cost of the road is based primarily on the terrain, how hard the road is to put in, how long it is, and how far away from the gravel pit you are. The gravel people will charge you for the gravel and hauling.

Now there are alternatives to this expense: first of all, you could plan a very short road and avoid the hassle, or if you want the privacy of a long road, you can put the road in yourself by clearing, excavating, leveling the road bed, and hauling the gravel yourself. Then all you'd pay for is the gravel. But let me tell you a startling fact. Gravel doesn't look like much, but a lot of gravel goes a little way. We have a bright-yellow former park district pickup truck that comfortably carries a load of one ton—beyond that the tires would pop or the axel would snap. And that one ton of gravel about half fills the back end. We bought one ton of gravel for around $1.25 and drove it back home to fill in some spring potholes in the road. We'd have plenty left over, we thought. Wrong. Fifteen little holes about the size of salad bowls just swallowed the whole lot. It seemed to sink into the mud and disappear. We kept shoveling and shoveling and poof, it was gone. With holes to spare. Okay. At that rate I'd guess that it would take us several thousand trips back and forth to the gravel yard before we'd get the whole quarter of a mile covered with gravel. Plus we'd have weeks and weeks of aching muscles and maybe $300 or $400 worth of just gravel. As I said before, a place with a good road already built is worthwhile.

If you still have your heart set on building your own shelter, I have one suggestion for solving your bare-land-no-road problem. Maybe it would be smart to buy an old, totally unusable house and its acreage, tear the house down, and salvage what you can from it. This way you'll save on building materials. You'll have some sort of water supply to work with; you'll have an overgrown road, but a road nevertheless.

Whether you buy an old place and move in, or buy an old tottering place, tear it down, and start again, there's one other thing you should know about roads. Living where they have a winter once in a while means you're going to have to plow yourself out. If one of your hopes is to find a "private place" where you don't hear or see any cars going by and where you can't be seen by the outside world, then prepare yourself for your long, long January road. Disappearing into the woods is beautiful in the summer. All you hear is the wind in the leaves, birds calling, insects buzzing, and a dog bringing in the cows at nightfall. But when you're stuck back in the woods in the winter, you can't hear a single sound of life. You hear absolutely nothing. And you can't see anything moving except the sun and thousands and thousands of miles of sparkling snow shifting places with the wind. Then suddenly your privacy isn't quite the treat you thought it would be.

To solve your snow problem, you can load up on mittens and shovels, you can buy a little plow, you can make an arrangement with a neighbor who already has a blade for his tractors (they call 'em blades; plows are for fields), or as a last resort you can pay the county or city to plow you out when they do the rest of the roads in the area. Sometimes, if you want to, counties will clear your road for free provided you legally declare your little private road a public road, allowing free traffic up and down it at any time. This seems a little self-defeating to me. You get this long long road so you can be alone and then turn around and declare it a public road that anyone can use, just to get it plowed. Peculiar logic.

WAIT A MINUTE

Back there a ways I made the statement that it's often cheaper to buy an existing farm than to buy bare land and build the place from scratch. I still think so. However, there are ways you can prove me wrong. It's possible, especially if you're willing to compromise a bit, to buy bare land, build shelter, water supplies, and everything else for much much less than you would pay for an old farm. First of all, you can buy fewer acres. And if you find twenty acres somewhere, or even five acres somewhere that are selling for $50 per acre instead of $300, you're halfway home. Finding these little plots is difficult because the country seller knows just exactly what you're about—he's seen or heard of the city people scrambling for country land

and he knows it's a seller's market. And if he's got a scruffy, untillable scrap of land on his property he may try to sell it for as much as the rest of his land is worth. Small plots of land in "sophisticated" areas are often more expensive per acre than large tracts of land per acre. But if you can find that inexpensive five acres, you have reason to be very happy.

If you're in solid with log-cabin building, earth ramming, sod, adobe, stonework, or cave living, you won't have to spend much money on materials for your shelter and can just gather them from the land you buy. Do the work yourself, buy nothing, and live handsomely. And if you do, you've really accomplished something, maybe of more value to your spirit than anything else you could ever do.

Should you decide to buy an existing farm, however, and apply your living principles the best you can, there are a few things you had better know. Don't buy an old house just for the spun sugar and romance. Buy one that's cheaper than you'd planned on and put the extra money into the changes you want or have to make. And, in spite of my earlier jabber about the economical old house, there are a few places lying around that would end up being very expensive even if someone gave them to you for free.

When you're looking at an old house, here's how to find out about the old gal's hidden body, secret thoughts, and weaknesses, how to really get into her and know her in one hour or less.

HOW TO JUDGE THE OLD HOUSE

If it's old it's got a few aches and pains. It may have tired foundations, headaches once in a while because of a leaky roof, or any number of ills caused by a few years of neglect. If you're sort of interested in having the old house for your own, start the relationship off right away with a personal question. Don't diddle around with small talk about lawns and planting and does the fireplace work or not, get right to it. "Tell me, how is the foundation?"

THE FOUNDATION

This is the most critical part of any house. Unfortunately, a bad foundation is not always going to stick out like a sore thumb. A weak foundation may be hidden in a number of ways: with paneling in the basement or ivy on the walls outside, but don't let it fool you. Before you do anything in this relationship, find out just how stable the house is. Don't make it your life's companion till you know it's solid where it counts. Here's how: take out a pencil or a little knife as soon as you can, go down in the basement and gently stick the pencil into the ceiling joists and beams. They're very obvious while you're standing down there unless there's been a false ceiling put up. (If there is a false ceiling, ask politely to have part of it removed. The seller or the broker, by the way, should never pooh-pooh your curiosity. They might be hiding something if they try to dissuade you.) When you stick the pencil or knife into the beams you should get a good solid resistance from the wood. If, however, you find the beams are soft and flaky and the wood sort of crumbles like old dusty cake, it's probably dry rot or termites. It's not something that you hide from a buyer, because it's a major weakness, a tragic flaw, and will be the house's downfall in the end,

Plastic foundations:

Anything plastic that you've been forced to buy can go in the bottom of the hole. Then pour in the cement. The plastic impedes the forces of frost.

because these beams are what hold the whole thing up. When they are weak, the whole house is jeopardized. Before you go much further, you can try to determine which it is: dry rot or termites.

Dry rot is really a misnomer; it's caused not by dryness but by dampness. Dampness from moist soil under the foundations or from wet floors is distributed in wooden beams by fungi that cause the destruction of the very fibers of the wood. Eventually the wood will be softened, seriously weakened, will show cracking, splitting, and will be crumbly. Termites do the same damage, basically, but they do it a different way.

Termites are a type of ant. But you can tell them apart from their cousins because a termite doesn't have a cinched-in waist like an ant and the little antennae that stick out from a termite's head are straight, while an ant has bent feelers. And unlike ants, termites think that wood is the greatest delicacy in the world. They'll come sniffing through the ground till they get a whiff of your old house's wood, and when they do they try to find an entrance so they can move in and stay for a very long supper. For appetizers they'll start on the beams and joists in the basement and then proceed through a zillion-course meal that includes wallboards, floors, stairs, windows—absolutely anything that's made of wood. And while they're chewing they make little mud-covered tunnels up the walls on their way to the wood upstairs. These tunnels are hard to see, but if you remove weather boarding or any kind of trim wood, you may be able to see them. Or, you can poke in the wood with your knife and maybe expose their highways.

Okay. Suppose, in getting to know the old house, you find decayed wood in the basement. What do you do? If

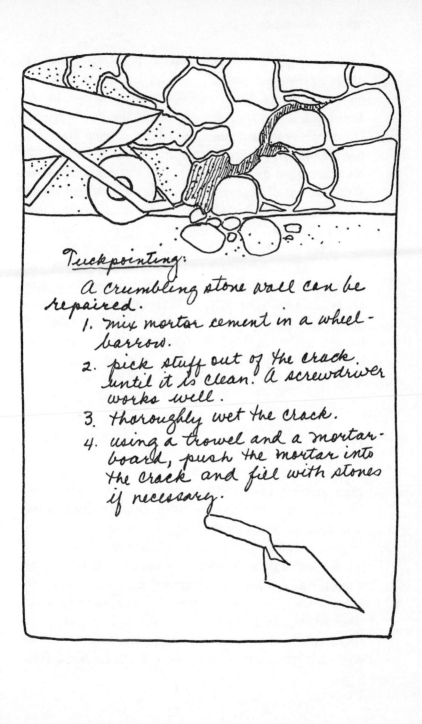

Tuckpointing:

A crumbling stone wall can be repaired.

1. mix mortar cement in a wheel-barrow.
2. pick stuff out of the crack until it is clean. A screwdriver works well.
3. thoroughly wet the crack.
4. using a trowel and a mortar-board, push the mortar into the crack and fill with stones if necessary.

you're young, choosey, and short of money, tell the seller it's been real nice and all, but you just don't think it's going to work out. Then, once you've said goodbye, leave. But if you're the type that can afford the great expense of a totally renovated house, bite down on your cigar and say, "Don't you worry about a thing, dear old house. I'll get you a good doctor and he'll give you a woodectomy. He'll take out all these old beams, supports, and bad wood, and he'll replace them with new steel ones. The best that money can buy. No, it won't hurt. It's expensive but I can afford it. And then after that, he'll go through every part of your masonry, and he'll see if he can plug up the spots where the termites get in, or where the water gets in. He'll check your attic, he'll check your rain spouts, he'll make sure that none of your wood parts are touching the soil. He'll run all kinds of tests on you and, my little rosebud, before you know it, you'll be in top shape. Don't be afraid, I'll take care of you. I'm very wealthy.

THE BASEMENT

Okay, now that you've found out the most important thing, and determined that the house is solid, stay in the basement for a few minutes more to take a look at the furnace. Now that's an optimistic statement. The furnace, in fact, may be upstairs in the kitchen in the form of a wood-burning stove or some other old-time warmth-giving gadget. And if it hasn't got a furnace, it's a safe assumption it doesn't have any plumbing either, because plumbing needs pipes and pipes freeze and break in the cold weather unless the house is heated throughout. Plumbing and central heating come and go together in old houses. But if the house does have a furnace, check to see that the ceiling beams just above it are protected by metal or asbestos covering. This way they won't catch on fire. After that ask the owner how much it costs to heat the house and then mentally add on $100 to the quoted figure. This is just in case the owner hates to think how much was paid to have a warm house last year and has repressed the actual figure or forgotten it. And it never hurts to overestimate your expenses by a little.

THE BATH

The house is "not modern" if the bathroom is outside. That means there will be no running water inside either, although there may be a pump in the kitchen. If you don't care about all that, fine. If you do want to put in plumbing, get ready for a basic cost of $1000 for fixtures that will be delivered to your door and left there for you to install. And consider $600 or more for a septic tank to handle sewage for you, not to mention the cost of a kitchen sink and a hot water heater, along with holes to be cut in the floors, pipes to be buried in the ground, and many many other little jobs too numerous to mention.

If the house does have plumbing, get to know the fixtures right away. Turn on a faucet and see how much water pressure there is. If it's drip drip dribble time, the pressure's not exactly exciting and may be due to pipes that are rusting shut or to some other factor, like water availability and pump capacity outside. Next is the flush. If it gurgles when it flushes instead of the regular roar, it may be missing a vent and you'll have to replace the plumbing system or get used to the smelly, unsanitary little closet.

Bill the cow dog is good
at getting the cows in or
out of the barn and pasture.
He barks and nips at
their feet. A good cow dog
never hurts a cow.

THE EYES

Take a look at the windows. They'll tell you a few nice things about how the house sees the world and how you'll see it if you live there. But more important, see how she blinks. If the windows slide up and down smoothly, that's good. If they don't, first look to see if they've been painted shut, and if it's not that, then prepare yourself for a disappointment. If the windows are jammed in a certain stare, it may be because the foundation has shifted and settled into a new lean. All the original horizontals and verticals in the house will be thrown off a little. So the window itself, which is square, will not slide up and down in a slanting four-sided space. Now what? About all you can do is go outside and look all around the walls for cracks, loose pieces, or dead bricks. If you find these things it's very likely the house has been thinking of moving away—hasn't quite decided when she's going to make the trip—but the trip is pretty much settled in her mind. And one day, when you and your friends are having the time of your lives, she'll simply announce her departure with a small creeeeeeeeek, and will slowly, gently gather her belongings and yours and move them all twenty-five feet to the east.

So, if the windows won't open, the doors won't close, the cracks in the foundation are obvious, don't buy the house. It's not standing squarely, it's balancing on one toe.

ELECTRICITY

More houses have electricity than don't these days; even

if they don't have bathrooms and furnaces, they do have electricity. So, when you're looking the house over, find out about its power. The main thing, of course, is whether it's old power or new. Old power, put in fifteen or twenty years ago, means that under that pretty exterior are hundreds of old wires, old wires that are conducting power to the plug, and power to the socket. And old wires can be dangerous—one bad fray and there's fire. Electrical fire spreads instantly along all the wires in the house and the whole place is burning all at once. It's not like catching a curtain on fire and having it spread to the window and then to the wall and then to the cupboard and then to the floor—it's almost instantaneous. An electrical fire is total fire in seconds. The floor, the roof, the basement, wherever there's electricity in the house there's flame.

Unless you're an expert, it's hard to tell how the wiring in the house is. But there are two things you can do. Take a look inside the fuse box in the basement. If it's real old-looking, chipped and rusty, and covered with dust inside and out you can be pretty sure the wiring is old, because when they rewire a house, they usually replace the fuse box as well, and in some areas put in circuit breakers instead of fuses. Also, while you're down there, see if the wires are exposed along the walls and ceilings, sort of strapped to the walls. This is a sure sign the wiring was done a long time ago because for the last ten years or so, wiring has been done inside the walls and is sometimes enclosed in a special little pipe that surrounds the works and prevents fire. Beyond these things you really can't tell much and you might need an expert to help you. You might just ask the owner how old the wiring is in the house. Sometimes people know and sometimes they don't. But if you get

Applesauce:
Peel, core, and quarter 4 or 5
apples. Bring to a boil in
1 cup of water, then simmer
till tender. Stir in ½ cup of
brown sugar and some dashes
of cinnamon and nutmeg.

an answer of twenty years old or so, definitely have it checked by someone. Don't throw in the towel on the house, but don't pay for it that very afternoon either.

Generations of people have survived successfully without electricity. They probably spent more time talking to each other at night than we do. They probably read less and got to bed earlier, too. In spite of the fact that it can be done, you may not want to do it; and if the house you like isn't equipped with electricity, here's what you should expect when you have it installed.

There are a lot of electrical codes that will dictate how you do it, and you have to comply with local regulations whether you wire the house yourself or have someone do it for you. When the wiring is done, there will be a lot of wall-cutting and hole-drilling going on and afterward a lot of replastering and repainting will be necessary. It could cost as little as $1000 if you find the right contractor, but if you have all kinds of bedrooms and parlors and kitchens and things to wire, don't count on getting away with just a thousand. The bigger the house, the more costly it is to wire. And then there's another problem. If your house is located any great distance from the power company, or any great distance from anyone else with electricity, you'll have to pay for the hookup. Power companies usually charge you a certain amount per mile and sometimes even break it down to a cost per foot for running wires to your house. It can be expensive. So the best thing is to get in touch with the man at the power company and find out when they can give you service, whether you'll have a hookup problem, and how much it will cost to wire your house. Then decide whether you can afford to buy it.

If your elm begins to lose its leaves on upper branches during the summer, the tree may have the Dutch Elm disease.

THE ATTIC

Whether there are stairs or a pull-down ladder, get up there in the attic next. Here you'll be able to see how it's been dealing with the sky and the weather over the years; how the man who made the house felt about details and solid construction; and how the owner generally has kept the house up. Laced between cobwebs, dust bunnies, stacks of old magazines, and pieces of unwanted furniture are several clues about your potential friend.

If the attic has been poorly ventilated, poorly insulated, or is leaky, it's possible that dampness has gotten into the beams here and caused dry rot. First thing you do is the old knife-in-the beams trick. As in the basement, if the wood is flaky or mushy it's a sign of dry rot or bugs. Check to see if there are windows at opposite ends of the attic or some other source of air; sufficient ventilation is a great way to avoid dry rot. Another thing to look for is insulation. If the house is rather old, it's likely the owner has at one time or another put insulation in himself. You'll be able to see it if he has. Either it's a sort of giant yellow sandwich type that's been nailed up, or it's the blown-type loose insulation. Loose insulation isn't too neat because it tends to pack and get lumpy and doesn't have a built-in vapor barrier like the sandwich type. It's just blown in there between the attic floor joists and into the walls, and it's not as efficient as the sandwich-type blanket or batt insulation.

Checking for dry rot and its causes—poor ventilation or bad insulation—is important. But there's one other thing to inspect while you're looking at the attic—the ceiling. If it's loaded with little patches of sky as you look up at it, you may have found another cause of dry rot.

Asparagus is a
perennial that comes
up in the spring.
The best time to cut
it is when it is
about seven inches
high and the tip
is still closed.
After this point
it is too stringy
to eat and
quickly goes to seed.

Sheathing is what forms the attic roof as you look at it. It's usually made of tongue-and-groove planks or big pieces of plywood stretched across the joists. It's there to seal off the house and as a place to nail shingles on the outside. The sheathing should be tight. Poor sheathing, or aging shingles on the roof outside, will let rain drip in; and drippy roofs not only imperil the wooden skeleton of the house, but also make watermarks on the ceilings and walls below. If the attic is littered with pans, you know what that means too.

Okay. Let's imagine the worst. The beams have dry rot, the insulation is lying in lumps everywhere, not a window in sight, there are holes in the roof and pans on the floor. What do you do? Well, just face it, you're going to have to spend a lot to fix it up. If you don't have the cash, forget the house—it'll get worse and you might as well not be living there while it does. If you can buy the place cheaply enough and have money left over to spend on repairs, then you'll have to replace the bad wood, ventilate the attic with windows, maybe reinsulate and definitely replace the roof.

The roof will be a major expense. The cost of reshingled roof is determined by the cost of the shingles, how many square yards the roof measures, and what someone will charge you to do the job. Get in touch with the local lumber yard; they usually sell roofing and can quote prices to you and suggest someone in the area who does good work. One thing to remember is that the more expensive the shingles are, the longer they're likely to last. If you get really good ones, you may not have to reroof for the next twenty-five years or so. That fact makes the higher cost for quality worth it.

You may want fireproof asbestos shingles or you may

Chickens lose
their feathers and
grow new ones
during the fall.
They are so busy making
feathers that they
don't lay eggs during
this period.

like the idea of the new seal-down shingles. Many manufac-
turers now make a shingle that you nail down just like
other types, often right over the old shingles, and when
the sun hits the roof, the back of the shingle melts a little
and glues it down and to the other shingles near it. This
shingle gives an excellent seal and won't blow up when
the wind is wild.

Whatever type of shingle you decide on, don't neglect
the metal flashing that runs along the eaves of the house
and prevents water from getting up under the roof and into
the wood of the house.

If you really love the house but find the attic in bad
shape, go ahead and buy. The attic and roof can be fixed.
It's not like loving a house with a bad foundation.

THE HEARTH

If someone showed me a hole in the ground that had
a fireplace in it and a place to sit in front, I'd consider
buying the hole. A lot of people feel this way about fireplaces
and will go to great lengths to have one, preferably one
that's all rough stone with a rising chimney right there on
the wall and a huge mantel made of a practically whole
tree. If you have a thing for fireplaces, here's how to figure
out whether that beauty in the parlor works or not.

Take some straw, wet it a little, and put it in the fireplace.
(You can also use paper, or anything that will burn and
smoke at the same time. Tarpaper is a great smoker.) Now
check to see that the flue is open, even if you have to
lean in and get an eyeful of soot in order to see the sky
up there. Then light the little pile and see how the smoke
draws. See whether the smoke escapes in little puffs from

orphan lamb

To get a mother ewe to accept
a new lamb that's not hers
is hard. The lamb doesn't
smell right. Some farmers
rub the ewe's udder ail on
the orphan's head. Some
get a dog to threaten and
the ewe will protect the
lamb and let it suck.

between the bricks or stones of the fireplace. If it's leaky, you'll have to fix it because it's a fire hazard to the rest of the house. You may even have to replace the stonework from the leak on up, because this leaky fireplace probably doesn't have a flue lining. A flue lining is the thing that protects the chimney stones from the gases of a thousand burning logs, the gases which collect on the masonry and disintegrate the stone bit by bit, all the way up the chimney. A flue lining protects the stone so you don't have to keep rebuilding the chimney.

If the fireplace is working and you've done your little smoke test, then check the outside of the chimney for cracks in the masonry. If everything is okay, hurray. Finding a solid house with a solid fireplace is fantastic. Buy it.

5

WATER

Thanks to 200 million consuming, peeing, thoughtless individuals in the country, we no longer have pure water in streams and lakes and rivers. Whole earth systems have been brought to a standstill in some places and replaced by a green scum. You certainly can't dip a tin cup in a stream these days without coming up with a mess of goo in it . . . or invisible bacteria, which is even worse, especially if you swallow it.

Drink wild water today, and you might get sick. Once you could drink anything, but that was when the Indians lived here.

This whole problem may have been the first thing which excited you about getting a little land, living in harmony with the earth, and being good to her. Ecology may be the issue that's sending you to the woods. But no matter how far you remove yourself from the ones you blame for the earth's coughing fits, no matter how much you change your ways and habits, the water's still in bad shape. Just because you think Indians had a great life and philosophy doesn't mean you can do it today. Just because people realize the water in our country is dying doesn't mean water can be saved by your moving to the country. Water won't get better just because people realize it's bad.

So with this fact in mind you should be very careful about your country water supply. Don't take chances because you believe in natural living. There's nothing natural in getting sick from bad water.

HOW TO JUDGE YOUR WATER SUPPLY

The next few pages are for when it's a sunny Saturday afternoon and you're looking at a farmhouse that really interests you. When you look at the place, you should be able to make some educated guesses about the water supply before you completely succumb to the old farm's loving. Make a good guess about the safety of the well or spring, and then contact some experts before you agree on a price. The guess is important and so are the experts.

Who's an expert? Here are a few:

1. The Health Department often has a water-testing lab located in the capital or at the state university. You write to them and they'll send you a sterile bottle and directions on how to take a water sample. Take the sample and then mail it back, making sure that the sample reaches the lab within forty-eight hours. They usually do this test for free and send you back a report on what they found out about your water.

2. Your county agricultural agent has the address of this testing lab, and sometimes the county nurse or the courthouse even has the bottles you need for your sample. Besides giving you the address of the lab, the agricultural agent has all kinds of information about water tables and recent ways farmers in that area have solved their water problems.

As I've said before, if you have any questions, ask the county agent—he's knowledgeable, his service is free.

3. The present owner of the farm can tell you a lot about the water supply. Get in touch with him if you can, or have the real estate agent ask him. If you've guessed that this water supply can't possibly be safe, and the owner says it is, be polite. You could be wrong. But make an excuse that, being from the city where water is such a problem, just for your peace of mind you'd like to have it tested. It's better to find out before you buy than after.

4. A local well contractor is another expert. Call him up and say that you're looking at a farm nearby. Tell him that you're thinking a new well might be necessary and ask him for information. He undoubtedly knows the particular problems of the area and will be able to give you a rough, unofficial estimate of how much he'd charge to put in a new well. This call doesn't commit you or him; it's just a good way to get a little more information.

5. Neighbors—that is, potential neighbors—can tell you their experience. What's true about water next door may be true about water on your property. Be tactful and polite to country neighbors; they are almost as important as the land you buy. And since that water question may be your first meeting with them, go all out to make a nice friendly impression.

Before you start rating and making decent guesses about the water supply on your place, here are a couple of basics about water and water behavior that will give you a feel for the subject.

Safe drinking water is described two ways: potable and palatable. Potable means it's safe to drink and palatable means it's safe plus tasty—with no funny odors, colors, or flavors.

Okay. Safe drinking water can come from two main sources: the ground or the surface. Ground water is water that's been trapped in a kind of underground stream called an aquifer, and an aquifer is what feeds your well or spring. To get to the aquifer, water passes down through numerous layers of earth; while it travels it is filtered and purified. The deeper down the aquifer is, the more layers the water passed through to get to it and the purer the water will be. Because it is likely to be purer, ground water is considered superior to surface water. Surface water is a pond, a stream, a lake, or a river that has just collected the water as it has dribbled through clouds or wandered down roads or hills. Surface water is not purified by the earth, and it is often polluted by people and their ways. In some states, it is against the law to use surface water for a domestic supply.

A well or a spring brings the water, the ground water in the aquifer, to you. And you can start checking out the safety of a particular well or spring by looking at the things around them. If you can see a cesspool, a big open hole in the ground full of sewage, an outhouse, barnyard, or other dumping area within fifty feet of it, beware. All these things have bad water seeping out or off of them, and that water will run right into your drinking water and wreck it. And, if one of these areas is located on a slope above your well or spring, the bad water will get in your water twice as fast. If the house has a septic tank, ask where it is. Septic tanks are buried in the ground, and they too should be at least fifty feet away from any water sources, preferably farther. If you can't see any of these polluters near your well or spring, one of your problems is solved. Now all you have to find out is the really hard stuff. What kind of well is it, or what kind of spring is it, and how

Trout like water 50-65 degrees and it has to be flowing and well aired.

We keep a few rainbows in the over-flow tank from our spring. A screen with big holes fits across the tank, so bugs can get in, but the fish can't jump out.

does it perform? Does it tap good water? Is it constructed well? Is it reliable?

SPRINGS

A spring is any place where the underground stream, the aquifer, comes to the surface. Usually it happens on hillsides or in the elbow kind of place where a hill hits a low spot. If it's a good-sized spring, near the house, it's likely the people built the house a long time ago to be close to the spring. They probably dug the dirt out of it, made a storage tank, put a little house over it, and used the water for drinking, cooking, and washing.

Not every spring has a spring house, though. You can spot a "wild" spring, a spring that people have never used, pretty easily just by the stuff that grows around it. Don't look for a torrent of cool gushing water. That often happens. Look to see if there are reedy, brown or yellowish kinds of grasses there, grass that's a different texture and color from the regular growth elsewhere. Willow trees are good signals, while cattails would mean swampy low ground rather than a spring. And, of course, if it's squishy ground all the time, that's a positive sign. If you stand back from the suspected spring, you should be able to see a pattern of different grasses sort of flowing away from the source, almost as though the grass were flowing like water.

If you're going to drink from a domesticated spring there are a few things you should check: the safety of the water, the reliability of the flow (you wouldn't want it to go dry some August afternoon), and how the spring has been kept up. Don't drink from the spring until you've had it tested, even if the family before you all drank it for years and never got sick; they may all have been immune to something you're not immune to—and also, after they did all that drinking, the spring may later have been polluted. That test will take a few days, but while you're standing right there on the spot you should inspect the spring house, the water tank, and the pipes. The spring house should be leak-proof because it is sitting right over the spring and is there to protect it from dirt, dust, leaves, rodents, and other animals. The water tank, or spring box, as it is called, should be watertight and have a tight-fitting cover. It should be, ideally, four feet deep or more, with part of that depth extending above the ground line. It can be bigger of course—the bigger it is, the more water you can store up. The spring box must also have an outlet pipe so that it doesn't overflow twenty-four hours a day.

After you've assured yourself that the spring is pretty well protected and taken care of, you should ask if it flows all year and how much water comes from it.

Here are some guidelines. Your spring or well should have enough water to supply each person twenty-five gallons a day if you have no indoor plumbing. But if the spring water is pumped and piped into the house so that a toilet will flush and a faucet will work, double the needed amount per person. You may find you need a lot less water, or you may need a lot more if you're very dirty people, very clean people, thirsty all the time, or go to the bathroom a lot. If you have livestock, you have to supply them plenty of water too. And their needs depend on the temperature outside, what they eat, and a lot of other variables like age and size, which you already know if you're in livestock, so I won't wear myself out trying to set it down.

The best time to measure spring flow rate is in the fall, when the water table is likely to be its lowest. You can estimate this yourself by diverting the spring's overflow pipe into a container of known volume. Measure how long it takes the spring to fill that container and then do your arithmetic to figure out how much water comes out a day. If the amount is less than you decide you need each day, then you'll need a storage tank put in.

One of the worrisome things about springs is that they're not really reliable. If they go dry because of some distant ground tremor, mining operation, or earth change, you can be in for a bad time. They can suddenly become impure if they are fed by a new stream of water that's been polluted somehow. Frequent testing is the best thing you can give a spring.

But if the spring is good, it's perfect. That infinite trickle of cool water rising up to you can fill you with a natural feeling you've wanted to have all these years in the city. You'll get the joyous emotion of being part of the land, part of the cycle of things as you lean over the spring, and feel the cool air brush your face as you dip your cup in. It's a beautiful feeling. It's a perfect spring.

WELLS

Many old farms have old wells. They work beautifully for many years, but don't necessarily work beautifully always. And yesterday may have been the last good day for that old well. So that you can make some guesses about the ones you see, I'll give you a description of the most common types of wells used in this country, some facts and figures to help you recognize the type on your land and evaluate its chances of serving you the way it should.

Earthworms feel
light. So they're
hard to catch at
night with a flash-
light. The worm,
however, can't
feel red light.
Shade your flash-
light with red
paper, walk
softly, and
catch enough
worms to fish
all the next
day.

Artesian

This kind of well doesn't need pumps or rams to deliver the water to you. The water flows up your well shaft because there's pressure below. The pressure comes from the weight of the earth above the water and from the contours of the land. If the source of the water is high enough in altitude, the pressure of the water flowing "downhill" will make it flow up your shaft and out of the earth. An artesian well is considered a very shallow well, it has to be in order to flow without pumps and since it's shallow, it's suspect. Not bad necessarily, but suspect.

Dug Well

This one starts with a man and a shovel. They dig until they hit water. The hole gets wider and wider, sometimes as much as twenty feet wide if more than one man did the digging. Then the walls of the hole are lined with concrete or tile or a very wide pipe and the diggers try to get out of the hole before the sides begin to fall in.

This kind of well has many drawbacks. If there are any rocks underground, the well usually can't be completed. If it can be dug, it has to be very thoroughly sealed in order to keep bad water from seeping in, and that's hard to do when it's so wide and rough. Consequently, the well is easily contaminated. The water in this well won't be as pure as water from a deeper well, and if you get a dry spell, this dug well is one of the first types to fail because it only goes down to the first level of water. There's one other possibility: since a dug well is undoubtedly an old well, that water may have been safe once upon a time, but time changes things. Not recommended.

Bored Well

Not as wide as the dug well because it's made with

an auger that removes the earth instead of by a man digging. If your soil is the kind that caves in easily, this sort of well can be trouble, just like the dug well. It too needs to be thoroughly sealed in order to keep bad water from getting into the shaft. A bored well is usually not found in rocky areas, or in land where boring is hard. One hundred feet is the maximum depth of this well, so if good water is 125 feet down, it's no good.

Driven Well

The skinniest well around: it's never more than two inches across. It's made by driving a lot of connected pipes into the ground, one on top of another, with a maul or a pile driver. The flow from this very thin well will be small, and if your land is sitting on top of rock or tough stone, you can figure your well is not a driven well. It is a shallow well, like the dug and bored well, and suffers from the same problem—it's fairly easily contaminated.

Jetted Well

Dug by pressurized water. This type of well is only possible in easy digging soil since rocks and nonporous layers can't be dug with squirts of water. If you have a jetted well on your place, it may be as deep as a hundred feet, and you should have it checked to see that the casing is still good. It's a fairly thin well, four to twelve inches in diameter, and it's not a really common one.

Drilled Well

The safest, most reliable well around by all accounts. It taps the purest water because it can go as deep as a thousand feet if you have to, and no earth formation can stop it. It's dug with heavy drill bits and stems that just pound and dig and force their way through anything.

If you find that you must put in a well because the old one is bad, you'll probably hear them say that a drilled well is for you. If it is, count on a basic cost of $1000 for the drilling, installation, and pumps. That's just an estimate because the price of your particular well is determined by the depth and difficulty in drilling it. Before you have the crew out there, though, get the contractor to prepare a contract form which says exactly what's to be done and how much it will cost. The contract should state that all work will fit county and state codes, and it should go into detail about casing specifications, well seal, test-pumping, and disinfection procedures. It should also include a date of completion and a test-pumping report, a guarantee of materials and workmanship, and liability insurance for you and the driller.

PUMPS

Pump types vary depending primarily on the depth of the well. If the well is less than twenty-two feet below the pump, then a shallow well jet or piston-type pump is used. If the well is ninety feet or less, you'll need a deep-well jet or piston type. A deep-well piston or submersible pump are used in wells that are more than ninety feet deep. These are rules of thumb, not absolutes, and the man who sells or makes the pump can give you the complete low-down on his special pump.

Along with the pump, you'll need a pressure tank that stores water for you so that every time you fill a water glass the pump doesn't have to start up again. Most pressure tanks have at least forty gallons' capacity and have automatic controls for the motor and the pump.

Love at night.
to call a friend,
lightning bugs blink;
crickets rub their
wing covers together.

The capacity of the pump should never be more than the well can supply. I don't know what happens if the pump's too strong—maybe you get a bathtub full of sand or rocks or something, and certainly your pump is totaled in the effort. Anyway, if there's enough water down there in your well, you might like a pump that pulls up three hundred gallons of water an hour. That way, you'll have plenty of water, enough for putting out fires and watering your crackley garden in the summer.

If your old house has an electric pump humming away, here are the main types; maybe yours is one of them.

Centrifugal

The shallowest of the bunch. It doesn't go great guns for wells much deeper than fifteen feet. But it's a pretty reliable pump nevertheless and gives a smooth, even water flow. If you're in need of a whole lot of extra water, this can be a very good booster pump because it doesn't have to sit right on top of the well in order to work.

Reciprocating, or Piston

For those of you who like to work for your water, this one can be adapted for hand operation. It works fine in both deep and shallow wells, and yields at a constant rate. It's easier to maintain than some of the other kinds because of the open cylinder at the very bottom of the well shaft.

Jet, or Ejector

If you live in a sandy area, it's not likely you'll have this pump because it is easily damaged by sandy water. Like the reciprocating pump, this one works well in shallow and deep wells, but below a depth of eighty-five feet it begins to lose its oomph.

Subermisible

Deeeeeeeeep. Pumps from depths of a thousand feet and gives a good flow to boot. If something goes wrong with this pump, however, it's got to be pulled from the well in order to fix it. A subermisible pump is like the jet pump in that sandy water wreaks havoc on it.

Submersible

Looks like the same name as the one above, but the letters are arranged just a little differently. And the pump is different too. For one thing, it will get along pretty well with sandy water. A submersible pump works in wells up to a thousand feet deep and can easily be frostproofed. Like the other pumps, its capacity depends on its design and the amount of power supplied to it. Recently, this is a widely used type of pump. Recommended.

Deep-well Turbine

Can pump huge amounts of water from way down there. You probably won't run into it unless you buy the municipal waterworks, or a big big farm that needs lots of water. It's a good pump, obviously.

Windmills

Windmills are probably the most natural and least wasteful source of power man has ever come up with, because all it takes is the wind to run it—no gas, no electricity; nothing burns or is destroyed. And a windmill can do lots of jobs besides pump water. It can be rigged to thresh grain, grind feed, run small electrical things like lights; it can even be rigged to saw wood. If you have a working windmill on your land, you'll grow to really love it. A little breeze will start the magic circle turning, drawing water up from

frogs and toads
spend the winter
sleeping in the
bottom mud of
ponds and lakes.

the well, making the metalish tune, like a strange prehistoric bird towering over you on long legs. Entertaining and working for you at the same time.

If you don't have a windmill on the land you want to buy, the best way to get one reasonably is to buy it used from a neighbor or friend. If no one you know wants to part with his, then you'll have to dig up between $500 and $2000 to pay for a new one. The difference in costs of windmills is connected to the size of the sails and the total weight of the structure. The bigger the sails, the more water that can be pumped, and the more expensive it is. And, if you're in an especially windy spot, the windmill and its base have to stay standing during a big storm. That's why you pay more for a heavier windmill. Get in touch with:

> The Heller-Aller Co.
> Napoleon, Ohio
>
> Dempster Industries, Inc.
> Beatrice, Nebraska

CISTERNS AND CATCHMENTS

The days of the old wooden barrel stuck in the ground are over, so if you have a cistern as the only source of water, you'll have more to keep you awake at night than just the thunder and lightning. A cistern is a lot of work and could be called a good way to get hassled on forty inches a year.

Before I get into the nitty-gritty of cisterns, their construction and maintenance, though, there are some delightful aspects to cisterns to my mind. First, they force you to conserve water. You don't just turn the faucet on and let it run while you chat on the phone—that would be disaster. You don't fill up the tub; you're careful of every single precious drop. You share tubs—which is nice. You have the softest water possible with cisterns, the kind of water that takes almost no soap and makes your clothes, your hair, everything smell nice. You don't have to jazz up cistern water with a lot of super-duper-strength detergents; clothes come clean when they've been washed in clean water. And best of all, cistern water is all rainwater.

The trouble spot in cisterns is not the pure rain, but the impure cistern accoutrements; you have to work to be sure they're as pure as the rain—and you've got to have enough rainfall to make all your work worthwhile.

The catchment is what most people call the roof on the house. The roof catches the water as it falls and leads it into a drainpipe through a series of filters, screens, and gutter guards, and finally the rain pours into the cistern itself, a big tank buried in the ground.

The area of the catchment has to be big enough to supply your water needs. That's the first thing. Then the catchment has to be kept scrupulously clean. It can have no bird droppings, dirt, dust, insects, or leaves stuck in the shingles because the grit will get into the cistern if you're not careful.

Now for the underground cistern. It should be large enough to hold water enough for three months or more—especially in areas where rainfall is scarce. It should be located far away from sources of contamination, such as outhouses, barns, and bad surface waters. It has to be watertight so that rainwater won't seep out or bad water seep in. If your cistern is superleaky, maybe a plastic liner or Portland cement paint would solve the difficulty.

One inch of rainfall
gives every acre of
land 100 tons
of water.

Cisterns also have a tendency to get scummy sometimes. An old farmer told me that he never let any rain in June, July, or August into his cistern and he never had a problem with scum in the cistern. I have no idea why this would work except that maybe in the summer bacteria can live on your catchment and in the cold weather they can't. Whatever the reason, this long abstention from rain gathering could cause some difficulty around the middle of August, but the farmer never mentioned that.

Don't drink cistern water unless you're absolutely sure the air the rain has fallen through hasn't been polluted, and that there are no bacteria on your roof and no leaks in your cistern. And all sorts of health departments say not to drink the water until you've poured some laundry bleach into the cistern after a rain. Laundry bleach works something like chlorine: it "purifies" the water, and the amount you use depends on the volume of the cistern.

Cisterns may be okay, but frankly, if there's another way to get water you might give it some long, tall, cool consideration.

PONDS

You can use pond water for drinking if you purify it first. The problem with ponds is that the watershed, the total land area that sends its rain and melt into the pond, is often beyond your control. Maybe a road runs through the watershed. Maybe a neighbor's field and his fertilizers will be swimmers in your pond. There are a lot of variables. If you are located in an area where none of these sources of pollution are threats, or if you own the whole watershed area, go ahead and plan your pond. You can get good advice and help in digging a pond from the agricultural agent in your county.

KA-KA POOEY, OR WHAT TO DO WITH SEWAGE

The most important thing about waste is to keep it away from any water sources—away from streams, wells, springs, ponds, and cisterns. Sewage can make you sick if it gets into your well or garden in a raw state. Take care of yours. It doesn't belong in streams where fish live and people dangle their feet. It doesn't belong in lakes and ponds. It's yours and it's your responsibility.

There are various ways that people have devised over a period of years to handle sewage, and you will find one or the other of them if you buy an established old farm.

OUTHOUSES, PRIVIES

An outhouse is a very good way to handle things—maybe the very best, ecologically; however there are different schools of thought, some saying it makes great compost after careful attention, others saying it clogs the earth's pores and is not a good earth procedure.

The earth-pit privy is the commonest type. A hole is dug in the ground and lined with wood treated with a preservative. Then the little house is built over the pit and the ground outside is made to slope so that rainwater will drain away from the building. If the pit is fifty cubic feet, five people can use it for as long as ten years before you have to relocate. To keep it nice and fresh, sprinkle some ashes, charcoal, plaster, sawdust, or dry dirt in there regularly.

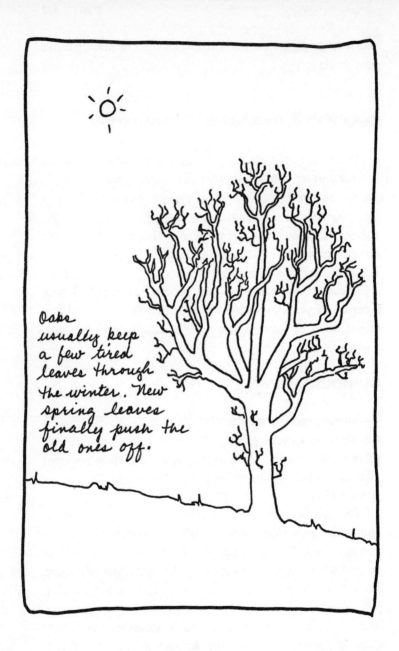

Oaks
usually keep
a few tired
leaves through
the winter. New
spring leaves
finally push the
old ones off.

The only thing wrong with an outhouse is that if it gets cold outside, you get cold underneath.

CESSPOOLS

These are illegal in many states, so you may never have the pleasure of seeing one. A cesspool is just a hole in the ground that lets raw sewage seep into the earth, sewage that is often carried to it in pails. The cesspool is not necessarily a covered hole—just a hole—and it's not a real swell way to manage things on a long-term basis because invariably the sides of the hole get plugged up and the sewage won't drain out and you have to clean the hole out. Enough said?

THE SEPTIC TANK

This is the way to take care of all that stuff if you have indoor plumbing. A septic tank is really nothing more than a tank buried in the ground that holds the sewage, lets it break down and settle out over a period of time, and then drains it out into an absorption field. It works slowly even though 98 per cent of sewage is just water, so the absorption field isn't overwhelmed. A septic tank works safely as long as it isn't located near a water source, and as long as you don't give it more than it can handle.

6

NEIGHBORS

HOW TO RENT YOUR FARM

Farms with livable houses are difficult to rent. It may have occurred to you that renting before buying is a good solution to your present lack of big funds, your lack of experience, or your hesitation to go whole hog on a country life. If you can find a farm to rent, you can indeed solve these problems, or begin to solve them, but the stumbling block is that a farm for rent is as rare as snow in July.

The main kind of renting that goes on in the country is for acreage alone. This fact won't help those of you who can't afford to buy a farm now, unless you can live on forty bare acres in a tent.

However, once you own land, renting out the excess acreage can be an advantage and a fairly simple thing to achieve.

One of the problems you'll have when you first buy a farm will be that you won't have time to do all the things your land may require immediately. Fallow, unworked land is a thing to avoid, and you may not have the equipment or the manpower to keep all your land active.

Inactive land sometimes gets restless, it isn't kept busy

growing crops or trees or grasses, and if its soil is left exposed to the elements it will blow or wash away. It takes a thousand years for nature to make one inch of topsoil, and it can take less than a year for the rain and the wind to move that one inch from your land to someone else's. Your unused land will leave inch by inch unless you take care of it. You can plant alfalfa, hay, or any number of other perennial plants on it; you can plant trees or reseed it into a pasture for animals. The roots of whatever you plant will lace the soil with a natural barrier to the erosive forces of wind and rain. As I said earlier, however, when you first move to your land you will not have time, probably, to do all the things that should be done. So the logical solution is to rent the land you can't presently take care of to someone who has the time and the means to do it for you.

Many established farmers are anxious to rent land. The most likely renter for your extra land will be the neighbor adjoining it or another farmer nearby. Approach them and discuss renting your land to them. If they are interested you should be able to tell them on what terms you will rent. Your county agricultural agent is a good man to ask for the going rental rate per acre in your area. Besides quoting the price you would like to receive for your land, you should also be able to tell the farmer how he can use the land, what crops he can and cannot plant there, and what methods of farming you will accept. The agricultural agent again is pretty good in agricultural techniques and will be happy to discuss what would be appropriate for your land with you. He will discourage you if you insist that your land be farmed organically, however.

When you rent to the farmer next door or down the

road, you should talk about everything you can think of with each other so that you understand each other's responsibilities clearly. This is the most important factor in renting. Don't start out with vagueness or misunderstandings. Once you've talked, a written lease is often the finalization of the agreement. The lease should include how long the land is to be rented and at what cost. It usually says that the land will be farmed in a "good and proper" way and that the renter takes certain responsibilities concerning buildings and fences, while the owner takes other responsibilities for materials to repair them. The lease may also state that you, the owner, have the right to break the lease if the rent is not paid or if the renter fails to live up to his agreements. You may contact a lawyer to help you draw up a lease and advise on state laws.

There are three main types of leases: a cash lease, a crop share lease, and a livestock share lease. You will most likely be interested in the cash lease, but for your information and understanding of the ways of the country, here is a description of all of them.

If you decide on a cash lease, you the owner receive a certain amount of money each year. The renter takes all the crop risks and also gets all the benefits if the crops grow twice as big as ever before. The renter takes the risks and the owner gets a flat rent.

A crop share lease is an agreement to share the crops grown on the owner's land, with an agreed portion of those crops to constitute the rental. Usually the owner's percentage is related to the fertility of the fields. In this agreement the owner often helps with the planting and harvesting of the crop and generally plays a much more active part in the growing. If the owner's machines are used, or if his participation is high, he may take the larger portion of the final crop. Obviously, the owner as well as the renter takes the risk of a bad year with this type of lease.

The livestock share lease is basically the same as the crop share arrangement, only there are animals or fowl involved. A percentage of the income from the livestock goes as rent to the owner, and if anything is grown on his land that doesn't end up in or under the livestock, the owner gets a share of that too. This type of lease gives the owner a more active role in the farmland than any of the other types. Simply put, the livestock share lease turns the renter into a sort of livestock manager for the owner.

Renting your extra land to someone makes sense. It protects land you cannot care for that year, and it has one other nice benefit for you. If you rent enough of your land, you will have your property taxes paid by the income. When tax time comes, you'll appreciate that.

FENCES

Your country neighbors will be trustworthy, generous, clean, friendly, helpful, courteous, kind, and reverent. Probably. If your neighbors are basically good people, it really would be unfortunate to get off on the wrong foot with them simply because you didn't know the ways and responsibilities of country neighbors.

Before you start the waving on the road or having long talks together in an alfalfa field, before you get anywhere near friendship, you should establish your good intentions with them. One thing that they'll be curious about is how you feel about fencing. Robert Frost's thing about "good fences make good neighbors" is very true, and although

the corner post

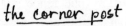

1. Set post in ground to the frost line.
2. anchor post by using wire stretched perpendicular to stress angles. Then attach wire to metal anchor that has been screwed into the ground about three feet away.

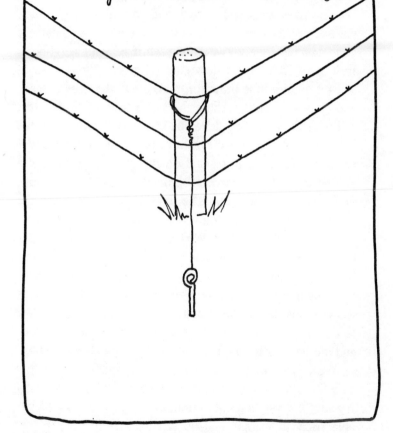

it may come as a disappointment to some of the total freedom lovers in the world, a good fence is a good start toward becoming more than neighbors.

Here are a few common accidents you can make that will put clenched teeth on your neighbor. All of them can be avoided by good fences.

1. You love goats. Their delicate, graceful movements around your land make you happy. Their milk and their cheese make you full. And, since you're not planning on keeping more than one or two, and you think they'll stick pretty close to home, you don't fence them. Then one day your dancing lovely ewe gets a whiff of your neighbor's fruit trees. She moves slowly away, gracefully as always, steps it up to a lithe little trot, makes it to the trees unseen, and begins nibbling. Ahhh, the sweet taste of apple bark. All over the trees this delicious bark. And, well well, the bark seems to be above eye level too. Just stretch a little, and eat. Not bad, just stand on my graceful hind legs a second and eat that bark all around . . . all the way up.

How cute? Not very. The trees are dead now and the neighbor's very mad. You should have fenced her.

2. Your dog is perfect. What a good dog. Loving, gentle, frisky good friend, your dog Tippy. Tippy in the country is the happiest creature you've ever seen. Running after squirrels that always get away and trotting out of the woods wagging his tail. Perfect! And it's really good not to have to take him out for a walk at night, to just open the door and out he goes for a good time, and you can keep reading.

While you're reading, Tippy's good time may be a few harmless pees around his territory, some sniffing and barking, but if Tippy's got it in him, or if Tippy meets undesirable friends, he may end up chasing cows or sheep that night. Running, they call it. And it's nothing like stealing

Goats don't eat junk. They're especially fond of root crops like carrots, turnips, and beets. Their milk is more digestable than cow's milk.

a couple of hubcaps. Dogs so terrify and panic domestic stock that once the chase is on, the animals run blindly, breaking steel fences, charging across the dark land, and finally, exhausted and skittish, end up five miles away in somebody's pasture.

Next day, the owner's out doing chores and sees his animals are gone. He sees the broken fences. In short, he is furious. He may be saying to himself, "Well, thank God they're not all piled up and smothered against a fence that wouldn't break, but I'll be goddamned." But the animals may be hurt and a broken leg is as bad as smothering in the long run. Your neighbor is going to wonder whose dog did this. Maybe it's that new folks' Tippy.

If it's Tippy, Tippy will get caught sooner or later cause Tippy will keep doing it. The farmer may catch him some night when he is carrying a gun and Tippy will be killed. It may be against the law—the sheriff is supposed to do this routine—but custom in the country says Tippy had it coming.

Some dogs have an instinct to herd, and perhaps that instinct carries over to this "running" thing. I'm not sure. But it saddens me to think of a good dog being killed because he has this instinct. If you have a dog that likes to chase, work hard to break him of the habit. Some farmers say it can't be done, but if it were my dog, I'd try as hard as I could to teach him. Unfortunately you won't have a lot of time. If the dog cannot be controlled, you'll have to take drastic steps: tie him, fence him, or give him a good home somewhere else back in the city.

3. Another irritant to a neighbor is your wandering bull. If you have a male animal other than a dog or a cat around the farm, you should make sure that he is confined. It's safer and it will please the neighbor. Animals that your

Bulls and steers.

A bull is dangerous. His sense of territory is strong and if you enter it, he's furious... he will get you out one way or another. If charged, strip as you run, drop your clothes and he'll "kill" them.

A steer is a bull minus his balls. Generally, he's not aggressive.

neighbor has are generally carefully bred for qualities which the neighbor believes will improve his farm's production, and he spends a lot of time planning for his herd and determining just when certain things are going to happen. If your bull gets into his heifer pasture, his virgin cattle are in for some nice times, but the farmer is going to be unpleasant about it. Probably your bull couldn't have timed it worse. Poor timing is almost as bad as an unacceptable bull to the farmer, and most likely your bull is nothing compared to the golden-balled stud service the farmer can get somewhere else or buy in a capsule. Keep your bull celibate, at least as far as neighbors' animals are concerned. Keep him fenced.

Fencing has a lot of purposes: keeping animals in bounds is the main one, and marking boundaries is another. Generally, adjacent farms have a fence at the line and custom has helped to solve the problem of who is going to take care of the hilly, woodsy half of the fence and who is going to get the clean straight half; naturally, it's easier to set or maintain a fence on clear ground. To decide who gets the easy half, the practice has been that the two neighbors face each other from their own land at the exact middle of their common boundary. Each is responsible for setting and maintaining all the fence to his right.

When you buy a farm, ask the seller how he and his neighbors have handled fencing. Most likely they adhere to this right-side rule, but they may have worked out another, equally fair solution. Go along with this alternative; it will save feelings and disagreements. You can be sure that the seller didn't want to do more than his fair share when they made the arrangement, and he knew the land better than you do now.

One other thing about fencing. It is not a wall. It is

Electric fences deliver a painful but harmless shock when touched. To test whether the fence is on, take a long weed and touch it to the wire. You'll feel a tingling through the weed if the fence is on.

not seen by your neighbors as your fortress. They feel free to cross the fence onto your land and extend the same privilege to you. If you want to walk in their woods, fine. If you want to cut their trees that's a different story, but walking is okay. If you want to toboggan on their hills, that's okay, but if you want to snowmobile, you should ask. The old golden rule works well in neighborly things: do to them as you would have them do to you, and you probably won't have any problems.

Getting along with your neighbors is easy if you remember these things. And if you're simpatico with each other, the next-door friendship can be a wonderful, trusting relationship. If your neighbor has a snow plow rig, he'll dig you out in a pinch. If one of his family is sick, you can take over a homemade casserole and some bread. Being neighborly is being thoughtful. One other nice thing about neighbors in the country: you don't have to be quiet. You can play your radio loud, twenty-four hours a day if you want to.

I remember a weekend when my family drove up to see us, and we all were enjoying the summer day, sitting on the porch in our jeans and workshirts, reading books, snapping garden beans, when up the road came our neighbors. They walked in twos and threes and with them came Grandma, various kids, visiting relatives and a big basket full of homemade, still a little soft raspberry ice cream, paper cups to eat it in, and spoons for everyone. A real ice cream social. I loved it. And it's nice having neighbors like this.

A successful farmer has to work seven days a week. He has to be part accountant, mechanic, businessman, veterinarian, carpenter, weatherman, and soil conservationist. Besides that, he is dependent on the whims of the weather, the government, and the laws of supply and demand.

7

FACTS FOR NONFARMERS

One of the hardest things to do in the country is talk to a neighbor about rural life. He's lived it—you haven't. So that you'll have at least a speaking acquaintance with your neighbor's basic knowledge, here's a gathering of facts and information that will not only get you close to the earthy things he knows intimately, but also be of real help in living your life in the country.

Alfalfa
This perennial plant has roots that go several feet down. It's used to feed animals and is cut off the land several times a summer; a process called haying.

Back rubbers
These are used to control flies on animals in the pasture. Often a back rubber is nothing more than a chain wrapped with burlap and strung between two trees. Periodically it is sprayed with insecticide. The animals get the idea and walk under it, rubbing the bug stuff on their backs and keeping the flies off.

Bees
Honey bees sting only once. Wasps, hornets, and yellow

If you've wondered how they fill a silo, it is done with a blower that attaches to a pipe on the side of the silo and goes into the top. The silage is then blown up through the pipe.

jackets can sting as often as they feel like it. You shouldn't be bothered by bees in the country if you keep in mind the fact that they are absolutely essential to the pollenization of almost every plant and fruit tree and flower that grows. Love bees; they hum and ignore you unless you scare them or get too close to their hives. Their honey is a good substitute for sugar in your diet.

Bird Goodies for the Winter

Besides filling up a bird feeder, you can attract your winter friends by making a real treat for them of suet and seeds and hanging it in a tree. Go to the meat department in the grocery store and ask them for chunks of suet. Get as much as you can; it'll probably be free, and it won't go to waste. Take it home and melt it slowly in a pan; pour it into an empty milk carton along with lots of seeds; and then dangle a twisted wire or a good strong twine with knots in it into the slowly congealing fat. Put the carton with its twine stem outside and it will get hard in five minutes. Peel the carton off and hang the thing in a tree near your window. Birds love it, and it's good for them. If you especially want to attract jays and cardinals in the winter, put extra sunflower seeds in the mixture.

Compost

Make a layered pile of every grass clipping, orange peel, leaf, or eggshell you have. When "garbage" is layered and combined with animal manure, nature's process converts them from rubbish to the most gorgeous garden soil you could wish for. Sprinkle your compost pile with water when you turn it every week or so, and you can't fail. If it gets smelly, cover it with a black plastic tarp. And when the vegetables and flowers in your garden get hungry, put some

Newer tractors with
wide-set front wheels are
more stable on hills
than the older ones with
front wheels that are
close together.

A baler picks
up hay that's
been drying in the
sun, forms it
into a bale, ties it
up in twine and
throws it out.

finished compost around their stems. They'll be healthier for your efforts. And the garbage of the world will be put to its best use.

Concrete

Concrete is measured by the cubic yard, which contains twenty-seven cubic feet. To determine the amount of concrete needed, find the volume in cubic feet of the area to be filled with concrete and then divide this figure by 27. The following formula can be used to determine the amount of cubic yards needed for any square or rectangular area:

$$\frac{\text{Width (feet)} \times \text{length (feet)} \times \text{thickness (feet)}}{27}$$

When making or ordering concrete from the co-op, add 5 to 10 per cent to your answer above to allow for waste and the thickness of the cement.

Cover Crops

Plants that you sow in the early fall, rake into the soil, and let grow till early spring are called cover crops. In the spring you turn the plants back into the ground, where they will add tilth and humus to the soil. The main virtue of cover crops, however, is that they send roots into the soil to hold it in place during the seasons when the elements do most damage to bare land. Heavy spring rains or fall winds won't hurt the field with a cover crop. Some good ones are: barley, buckwheat, cow peas, millet, winter rye, sorghum, clovers, hairy vetch, and winter wheat

Crown Vetch

A plant recommended by experts to stop serious soil erosion. If your land is being chopped up by the elements,

Manure is aged and spread on the fields as fertilizer primarily during the winter and early spring. A spreader throws the manure evenly over the ground.

A farmer's plow prepares the soil for planting. A 4 bottom trailing plow has 4 tines which are pulled behind the tractor.

People move snow in the country with a blade, not a plow.

if you see that a gully is getting deeper every time it rains, you must take steps to slow the loss of your precious topsoil. Crown vetch is a good plant to put in, but actually any vegetation that can take root will do. The point is to bind the soil together with an elaborate root system. Even a layer of mulch will alleviate the problem temporarily.

Cucumbers

This vine is the most incredible grower. When your packet of seeds says plant 6 to a hill, do just that, and if you are a family of not more than 6, plant one hill, pull half of them out after sprouts appear, and you'll have enough for a cucumber morning noon and night, plus thousands of pickles of all sizes. Cucumbers will take over your garden if you let them or if you overplant.

Culling

A farmer who raises animals or birds for a living has to do this occasionally in order to maintain a healthy herd or flock. He weeks out the non-producers, the old and the weak, and sells them. This way he ensures a healthier, younger herd and a more profitable business for himself.

Dressed Weights of Slaughtered Animals

Cattle	*Percentage*
Dairy cow	40–50
Prime cattle	60+
Average for cattle	55

Sheep	
Wide range	40–65

Average lamb............................48–52

Hogs
Prime heavy 82–84
Medium 78–80
Shipper hog 72–76

Chickens
Cocks....................................76
Hens 76
Pullet (young hen) 74

The Farmer's Co-op

The co-op in your town is a source for everything, including heating oil, seeds, tools, cement, furnace repairmen, bone meal, garden supplies, and hundreds of other things and services. You buy at the co-op and can get goods at cost plus a little to cover expenses, and if the co-op makes a profit at the end of the year, all the people who bought there get a share of it, the share depending on the participation.

Feedlot

An area where animals are fed. It is a substitute for pasturing pigs, cattle, or whatever. And, according to modern farming methods, it is a more efficient way to provide the animals with exactly the food they need at their period of development. Feedlots are a more efficient but less natural way to run a livestock business.

Fire—How to Prevent It

Keep weeds down around buildings, especially in the fall, when it's likely to get dry outside. Never smoke in a barn; there's nothing there that won't burn easily except

A planter digs the
furrow, drops the seeds
in at the right interval,
and then covers the
seed up with soil,
all in one operation.

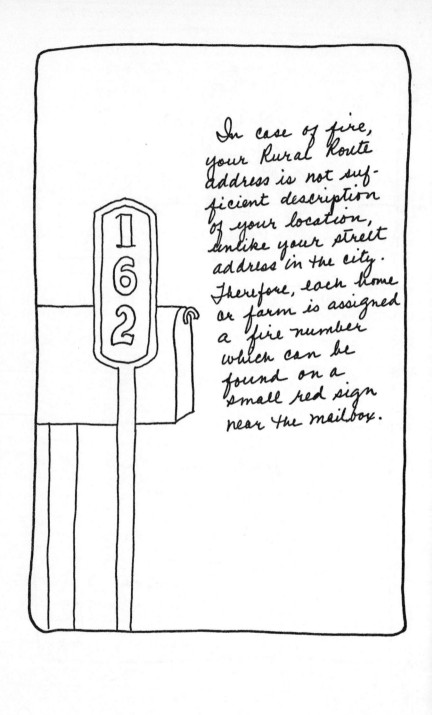

In case of fire, your Rural Route address is not sufficient description of your location, unlike your street address in the city. Therefore, each home or farm is assigned a fire number which can be found on a small red sign near the mailbox.

the foundation. Have extra hose attachments that can reach from your outlet on the house to any building you value. Dig a pond, and you'll have water in an emergency.

Freshen

A term used by dairy farmers to mean that a cow has just given birth to a calf and is now giving milk again. She will give milk for nine or ten months after calving, then by milking less often, the farmer dries her up in anticipation of another birth which the farmer instigated months earlier. The cow must be "bred back"—that is, impregnated—shortly after each birth to continue the cycle of birth and milk.

Frost

The superman of nature, frost can bend or break anything man can make, including steel. With continued freezing air temperatures, the water in the soil turns to ice and consequently the soil expands, putting constant pressure against everything it touches, be it roots or foundations. Foundations which are not set below the frost line—the depth to which the ground freezes—will buckle, heave, or sink with the terrific force exerted against them, and you'll discover the damage in the spring. Frost lines vary from place to place, and you should ask a neighbor what it is in your locality. If you build a foundation for a building, be sure to set it below the frost line.

Garden Planting Distances

Plant	*Distance Between Plants*
Beans, bush lima	6–8 inches

Beans, bush snap 3–4
Beans, pole snap 6–8
Beets 2–3
Carrots 1–2
Chard 8–12
Cucumbers 10–12
Kohlrabi 3–6
Lettuce, leaf 3–4
Mushrooms 10–12
Onions 2–4
Parsnips 3–6
Peas 1–2
Pumpkin 15–18
Radishes 1–1½
Rutabagas 6–8
Spinach 2–3
Squash 15–18
Sweet corn 10–12
Turnips 3–4
Watermelon 24–36

Gate
Never open one without closing it behind you.

Gestation Periods

Bear .... 6 months
Dog .... 63 days
Cow .... 9 months
Cat .... 63 days
Deer .... 8 months
Goat .... 5 months
Horse .... 11 months
Mule .... 12 months
Rabbit .... 30 days

Sheep ....5 months
Pig ....16 weeks
Squirrel and rat ....28 days
Wolf and fox ....62 days

Gilt

A young female pig that has not had babies yet. Cattle in the same condition are called heifers.

Green Manure

A plant grown for the purpose of tilling it into the ground in the spring. It adds nitrogen and other needed nutrients to the soil.

Groundhog

This furry brown creature waddles around looking like a lovable small dog, even though there's a trace of rat in its face and tail. A groundhog is nothing to worry about unless you find he or she has been digging burrows around the foundation of a building, especially a barn or a house. The groundhog hibernates and, come fall, the burrowing time arrives and the animal looks for a nice solid thing to dig its hole near. It likes to cuddle up to foundations when it's sleeping in December. You should not allow this because the burrow winds underground, zigzagging along the outside wall of the foundation, and becomes filled with fall rains and extra amounts of moisture which then freeze in the winter. The ice is concentrated along the foundation wall and exerts a powerful force against it. The foundation can be pushed inward, causing the building to ultimately collapse.

An old-timer will advise you that you must get rid of the groundhog—and the only way to do that is to sit near its hole, wait till it comes out for a breath of fresh air, and pick it off with your .22. If you say you don't want to do that, he'll suggest that you buy a trap, bait it, and when the thing is caught club it to death. This trap sometimes catches cats and other small animals. If you say you don't want to do that, he'll suggest getting a Have-a-Heart trap from the Sears catalog, but if you don't have eighteen dollars to spend on a trap and wouldn't know what to do with the groundhog once you caught it, here's another solution. Get a gallon of creosote (a wood preservative) and a pipe about three to four feet long, and stick the pipe into his holes or pound the pipe into the ground till you've hit a tunnel; then pour in the creosote. Make several pours in different places near the burrow. The creosote smells so awful that the animal will find his burrow uninhabitable, will leave and not come back. Be sure to then fill the holes thoroughly with dirt and pack it tightly down again.

Hay, make it while the sun shines

Making hay is nothing more than cutting a plant off the fields and taking it to the barn for storage. Farmers have learned from experience that making hay at any time when the weather is damp can be dangerous. Wet hay stored in a barn gives off gases and heat and the danger of fire in the barn is high. Therefore, farmers say, make hay while the sun shines, meaning, Don't take wet hay into the barn.

Heat, Duration of Farm Animals

In Heat	If Not Impregnated Heat Will Happen Again in
Mare .... 4–5 days	3–6 weeks
Cow ....12–24 hours	3–4 weeks
Ewe (sheep) .... 1–2 days	17–28 days

Sow............... 3–4 days   21 days
Often when you see blood, it's too late.

Hog wallow

Contrary to popular opinion, pigs don't wallow in goo all day. But on a hot sticky summer afternoon, a pig has frequently been known to enjoy a quick dip in the mud. It cools them off and keeps little insects like mites and lice off their backs. A hog wallow is a place where the pig does it and sometimes the wallow is portable so that the farmer can move it from place to place, depending on the pigs and the weather.

Incubation periods

Chicken...............................21 days
Ducks ....30 days
Guineas..............................28 days
Geese ....30 days
Pheasants...........................25 days
Pigeons ....21 days
Swans ....42 days
Turkeys..............................28 days

Land Measurements

A township is 36 sections, each a mile square.

A section is 640 acres.

A quarter section is half a mile square—160 acres.

An eighth section is half a mile square, north and south, and a quarter of a mile wide—80 acres.

A sixteenth section is a quarter of a mile square—40 acres.

The sections are numbered 1 to 36, starting at the northeast corner of the township.

Land Measure Trick

The number of acres in a body of land can be figured by multiplying the length by the width (in rods) and dividing the product by 160. When the opposite sides of the area are unequal but parallel, add them and take half of the sum for the mean length or width.

Lightning

In a thunderstorm one bolt of lightning will strike about every sixteen acres. To say it another way, lightning will strike one square mile of land forty to eighty times a year. Besides being an oak-splitter, TV-set-popper, and barnburner, lightning strikes people as well. It is a danger in any rural area. Lightning is the sort of creature that tends to take the shortest distance it can from cloud to earth, and any isolated or tall object that might ground it will attract it. To avoid being struck down by this sometimes 100 million volts of pure energy, there are a number of things you should do. When you are outside in a thunderstorm, stay away from fences; they are connected metal conductors and if struck even miles away can bring the electricity to you in a split second. Even if you are not touching the fence, the lightning can jump to you. You probably know the other cautions, but I'll repeat them. Don't carry any metal objects with you—no fishing poles, no fence posts—and don't sit on or under a tractor. If you are outside, the safest place to be is in the middle of a field. Crouch down in the open away from trees at a distance exceeding their height; get wet, but stay alive.

Along with your own safety, you should make sure that

all the buildings you value are protected as well. A good lightning system, regardless of make, size, materials, or construction will have six basic parts.

1. Air terminals, or rods, at least ten inches high should be spaced every twenty feet along the roof. 2. Conductors made of copper or aluminum cable should lead to the ground from the lightning rods. 3. Tie-in cables should connect all water pipes, siding, and other metal objects to the main ground. 4. Arrestors should be mounted on electrical wires and cables. 5. Grounds or metal rods should be sunk at least ten feet into the earth at opposite ends of the building. 6. The UL label signifies approval of the electrical product by the Underwriters Laboratory.

Lightning, like everything else in nature, serves a real purpose; it isn't there to just make people worry. Lightning brings nitrogen from the air to the earth by converting it to an oxide, which then falls with the rain to fertilize the soil. Along with earthworms, humus, and manure, lightning takes part in the nitrogen cycle and helps to continue the pattern of life on earth.

Logging
If anything is dangerous for the novice in the country, it's cutting down big trees. You can be killed by one miscalculation. I recommend that you hire someone in the area to cut trees for you. They'll charge you for it or haul it away and pay you a percentage of the price they get for the wood if they sell it to a lumber company.

Mailboxes
Your rural route address will require putting up a mailbox by the road. Check with the post office in town for the height the box must stand above the road, and the distance

it must be from the side of the road. And by the way, the red flag is put up by you when you want to signal the postman that there is a letter inside to be mailed.

Money, Ways to Make a Little

1. Set up a roadside stand with your pickup truck and a canvas or a simple shelter by the road. Organic home-growns are good for people.

2. Open a little store in town and sell things you've made, or teach people a craft.

3. Start a small mail-order business with items you've grown or made. Imagination and personal attention are the most important things here. Next to what you're mailing, of course.

4. Fifty chickens will give hundreds of eggs. Enough to supply the local grocery and you.

5. Dry some homegrown weeds or flowers and drive to a nice store in the city where they'll sell like mad.

6. Make holiday ornaments from things that grow near you. Send them out mail order.

7. Make candy.

8. Grow mushrooms in your cellar and take them to town. It's probable that they don't have mushrooms except in urinary-looking jars, and they'll like yours better.

9. Make honey. Bees are also good for growing things.

10. Make furniture and sell it out of your barn.

11. Grow worms and sell them to fishermen.

12. Be a blacksmith.

13. Whittle things, carve things, make woodcuts and sell them.

14. Grow trees for timber, nuts, or Christmas orders.

15. Sell teas made from your flowers and herbs.

Mulch

Surround plants with
leaves, straw, peat moss,
or any other organic gathering.
This mulch keeps soil cool
and moist and later decays
into soil, making it richer.
Mulching cuts weeding
a lot and gives a nice bed
for vegetables to rest on
when they're ripe.

16. Make candles and see if the drugstore man would let you sell them in his store on consignment.

17. Make pottery.

18. Weave and use your own sheep's wool.

19. Have a lemondade stand in the summer, and make it right before your customer's eyes: Quarter a lemon; crush it up in the bottom of a big glass with a potato masher or rounded piece of wood. Pour in enough honey to sweeten (a tablespoon or so); add ice and water to the top of the glass. Cover with the glass you're going to serve it in and shake. (If it's booming, get your lemons wholesale.)

Make anything you're good at and like to do. Macrame, knitted things, homemade leather things, quilts, baskets, bird feeders, dill pickles or pickled peaches, jellies, jams, toys out of socks, pillows, place mats, sculptures, refinished auction bargains—there are all kinds of things I can think of that I'd like to do, and I'm sure you could add to the list. The important thing is that it be something you like to do and, secondarily, something that someone, somewhere, will want. It's safe to say that handmade things, good fresh food, and old-fashioned honesty and skill are gradually being sought by the majority of people in this U.S. of A. And if you open a little store or put want ads in appropriate magazines or write a little article about your efforts to a big-city newspaper, whatever you do to attract customers or mail orders, you'll be surprised at how quickly you can be busy selling your treasures.

One maxim, if I may: Always give people more than they pay for. They'll come back for more, and you'll like yourself.

Money, Ways to Save It
Use clouds instead of TV.

Don't throw out chips of wood. Burn or whittle.
Cut down on the electric cords in your life.
Make toys from leftovers.
Make do.
Living is making.

Mud

In the early spring, the sun and warmer weather melt the snow and thaw the top two or three inches of soil, but below that level the earth is still frozen solid. Mud happens because the melt water and frequent spring rains can only be absorbed in the ground as far as the ground has thawed. And this is the time when your soil is in the greatest danger of being eroded, because water is intensified on the small but very important surface soil. Until the ground thaws you will have mud. By the way, when driving through mud, the secret is to go slowly; you'll have better luck and less chance of being thrown into a deep rut made by another car or truck.

Noxious Weeds

Most states have noxious-weed laws which hold the land owner responsible for the eradication of undesirable or highly prolific plants. Most landowners make partial attempts to get rid of weeds that affect their crops or their comfort, leaving the rest of the culprits growing where they are. Among the plants called noxious weeds are marijuana and daisies.

Organic Soil Testing Lab

Bio Chemical Research Lab
Threefold Farms
Spring Valley, New York 10977

Send these folks a good-sized sample, say one or two cup-fuls, tell them what you plan to grow in the soil and as much history of the ground as you can gather. They'll send you a report on your soil's characteristics and needs.

Pipe
Double the diameter of a pipe and increase its capacity four times.

Posthole Digger
Besides the regular tools you'll need, shovels, wheel-barrow, scythe, hammer, and so on, a posthole digger is a real helper. It looks like two shovels put together so they face each other. The digging end is made of two long and slightly inward-curved pieces of metal. You use it for putting in fences, but we found it a good all around digger. We plant trees with it. The secret of using the posthole digger is this: Don't lean your weight on it like a shovel when you dig; your shoulders and back should stay out of the work. Throw the thing at the ground with your arms, then twist the two handles, pulling them apart so that the shovels at the end pinch together, and pull up a big chunk of soil.

Pruning
There are thousands of books and opinions on when to prune trees and how to do it. As a rule for beginners who aren't making a living off the trees, however, it's safe to say that when in doubt, prune. It's better to prune than not to in most cases. Pruning has many purposes: to remove dead branches, thus giving the living ones more juice to grow; to remove splitting or overweight limbs, thus making the tree more safe to walk under; to lower the crown and

encourage side branching; to balance the top of the tree after a root injury, especially at time of planting; and to shape the tree. When pruning just follow these simple rules. Never cut all the branches in the middle of the branch; cut a few of them at the trunk, being careful not to wound the main trunk. Make two cuts perpendicular to the branch you're removing, about two inches from the trunk, then make a clean cut of this stub right at the outside of the trunk. Paint the wound with a tree compound made for the job. When trimming upper branches make a slanting cut, not a straight-across one; don't paint it. The branch will live and probably form several branches at the cut.

Purple Martin

Pretty birds that are very particular about their houses and eat a thousand mosquitoes a day.

Quack Grass

This weed is the one I really dislike. Dandelions, prickly things, and all the other ones I can handle, but quack grass is an unrelenting, clever, and fast grower. The long shooting roots of this one branch out in every direction, grow at amazing speeds, and send up another wide-leafed grassy-looking plant at every half inch of root. It can take over your garden, your asparagus patch, or any other place that's got exposed soil. Mulching, even six inches deep, does not discourage it much. It just grows. The only cure is a halfway one; you'll never get rid of it. You just have to keep yanking at it, pulling it up by its foot-long roots, and doing the whole process again the next day. You can buy a chemical killer for it, but I prefer not to jeopardize my organic garden.

Rabies

The animals most likely to get rabies in the wild are skunks, foxes, and squirrels. If the animal is sluggish or acts unnaturally tame, don't get near it. It will bite because it is sick.

Rats

One ratty couple can make 1500 baby rats a year. If you see a rat in your buildings, the saying goes, you can count on twenty unseen ones. Rats are most noticeable in the fall, when they start hanging around buildings to avoid the cold, and in the spring, when they run back and forth from their homes to the fields where new green things are growing. If you see a rat at night, it shouldn't worry you too much because rats are nocturnal things, but if you see rats during the day, they're probably crawling the place. Well, what to do about them? You know already that rats will spoil grains, spoil anything you intend to eat, and are just plain nasty disease carrying creatures. Get rid of them as best you can. Don't leave food around unless it's in a metal container, or a can with a lid; a rat will chew through a cloth sack in a flash.

There are several ways to kill rats. You can buy a poison at the hardware store called D-con; it looks like grated parmesan cheese, but when they eat it, it acts as an anti-coagulant in their blood. They begin to feel very hot and will seek a way to the outside, where they will die quickly.

Another way to get rid of them is to drown them, but first you have to gain their confidence. Put some boxes up against the wall in the building where the rats live and place a big barrel next to the boxes with some feed in the bottom. The barrel should also have a piece of wood stuck vertically in it. The rats can get in the barrel easily by climbing on the boxes, and after eating the feed they can get out by climbing up the stick. Let this system stand for a few days until all the rats in the building have tried this free lunch and know it's there. Then one night, take the stick out of the barrel and fill the barrel with a foot or more of water. The rats will jump in the barrel thinking they're going to eat, but will drown instead.

Riveting
If you rivet something doubly, it is 16 to 20 per cent stronger.

Roof Area
One hundred feet of roof area, with shingles four inches to the weather, requires about a thousand standard shingles and five pounds of nails.

Runoff
In hilly areas, rain and melting snow can cause deep gullies in the fields and along roads. You should learn the ways of seasonal water and dig trenches to control where it runs. You can save yourself the expense of having to regravel and resurface your road, and you can preserve the topsoil on your land with a little hard work and a shovel.

Russian Olive Trees
A hedge-sized plant with silver leaves that attracts more birds than a tree ten times its size. Russian olives have berries the birds can't resist.

Seeds
If you buy a packet of seeds for your garden, but don't use all the seeds, don't throw away the extras. Although

When in doubt, plant
a seed at a depth
of four times its
diameter.

the packages usually says something like "packaged for the year 1974," that doesn't mean the seeds will only grow in 1974. Seed companies usually state what percentage of the seeds in the packet will germinate, and they make that prediction once a year. For instance, they may take a sample of the radish seeds they have, throw in the seeds that were returned unsold by the stores last year, and plant them. They figure the germination rate by counting the seeds that sprouted and those that didn't. Then they repackage the radish seeds for 1975, state the germination rate, and sent them out to stores again. So save your seeds. The only thing that will happen to them is a gradual decline in the germination rate.

Septic Tanks

Most localities have health regulations concerning septic tanks, the main concern being that a septic tank be installed in soil that's appropriate for its safe operation. Check on health regulations before you install a tank. Generally, your septic tank should have a minimum of 500 gallons of liquid capacity, a baffled outlet, and not a single leak. If your tank serves more than four people, you will have to increase the capacity of the tank proportionately; for six people make it 600 gallons; for eight, 750 gallons; for ten, 900 gallons. The tank should be inspected periodically and should be cleaned when the sludge takes up half or a third of the liquid capacity. The scum and sludge taken from the tank should be buried way far away from the homestead; otherwise it can contaminate water supplies with its active bacteria. I recommend having an expert do this cleaning job for you; it's ucky and must be done perfectly in order to be sanitary.

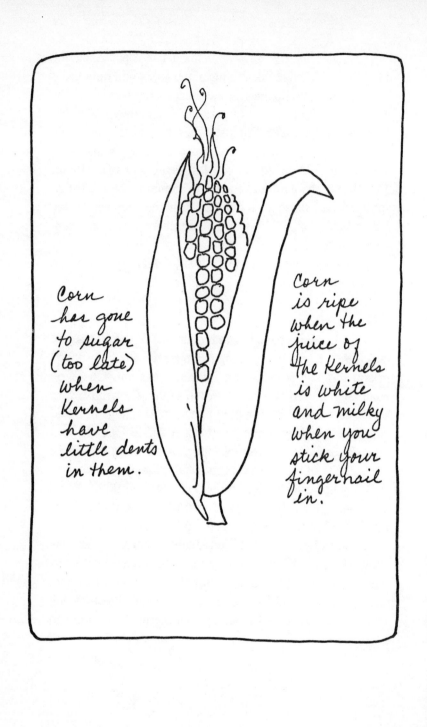

Corn
has gone
to sugar
(too late)
when
kernels
have
little dents
in them.

Corn
is ripe
when the
juice of
the kernels
is white
and milky
when you
stick your
fingernail
in.

Soil composition

Soil is made of inorganic things like sand, rocks, and clay, and organic things like decaying grass, plants, and animal manure. In order for plants to grow in it, soil needs to have a supply of phosphorus, potassium, and nitrogen built into the inorganic and organic bits that make it up. How much of each of these depends on the type of plant you want to grow and its needs.

Soil Tests You Can Do Yourself

You can order a soil-test kit from many people. I'm happy with mine from the Sudbury Laboratory in Sudbury, Massachusetts 01776, and it cost about six dollars. They'll send you the magic ingredients, bottles and corks and instructions to test your soil for its nitrogen, potash, and phosphorus content, as well as its alkalinity or acidity. From the test you can figure out what and how much you have to add to your soil to make it better.

You can also tell something about your soil by just looking at what grows there naturally. Dark-green plants grow in good soil, usually. Trees with branches that droop (except willows and other regular droopers) are hungry trees. Pine and blackjack trees grow in poor, acid soil. Plants seek their favorite environment and some plants thrive on bad soil.

Get your city fingers dirty and dig up a handful of dirt and squeeze it. If it's damp and sticky and you can make a ball of it, you have a lot of clay in the soil. Clay soil doesn't look crumbly; it has a red-yellow tinge to it. If the soil is powdery, there's a lot of silt or sand in it. A mottled yellow-gray soil may have had a lot of water standing on it which has leached out some nutrients. But if it crumbles

may: asparagus
june: strawberries
july: tomatoes
aug: corn and melons
sept: apples and grapes
oct: pumpkins

like dry black bread and has breakable clumps in it, it might be pretty good soil.

Get an empty pickle jar, put a handful of soil in it, fill it with water, and shake it, baby. You're going to find out just how much clay, sand, and silt are in your soil. Let the stuff sit for a few minutes and watch it settle out. The sand will drop to the bottom right away, then the silt drops out on top of it, and at last the clay settles.

Soil that drains well is good soil, it takes water easily and lets air in as well. You can test how well your soil drains with a coffee can that's had both ends cut out. Push the cylindrical can into the ground about two inches and fill it with water to the top. Sit down and watch. This may take a while so if you want to bring your harmonica and practice, that's okay. After one hour is up, measure how far the water has dropped from the top of the can. If it's three inches, you've got soil that drains very well; if it's one to three inches, that's pretty good; but if it's less than one inch you've got soil that's too tight, it doesn't drain well, it isn't permeable.

Sprouts
Never sprout seeds for eating that are intended for planting. Bean sprouts and all the other favorite crunchies will be better if you buy seeds that are intended to be sprouted. The regular planting seeds are sometimes coated with protective things that are not intended to be eaten.

Steam
Steam rising from water at its boiling point of 212 degrees F. has a pressure of 14.7 pounds per square inch.

Storm Warnings
A storm is likely if you see leaves turning their silver

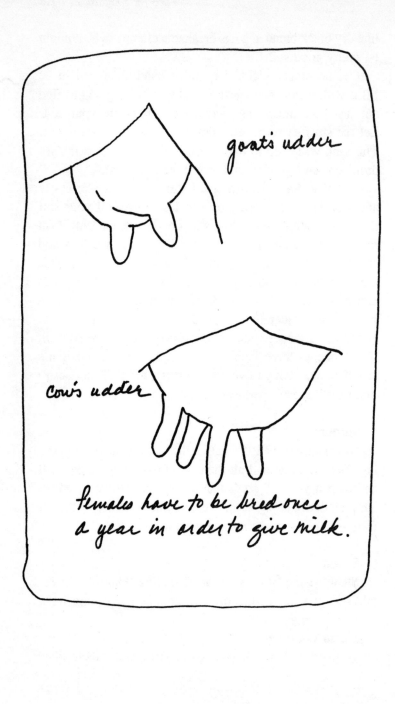

goat's udder

cow's udder

females have to be bred once
a year in order to give milk.

Farm Soup

1 short rib
1 t. vinegar
1 t salt
big pot of water

boil till 1 inch of
water is left.
Remove bone and
return meat to pot.

any vegetables
currently growing
in your garden

wash lightly,
B vitamins are
water-soluble.
Cut in chunks
and put in pot.

tomato paste
and fresh herbs
as you like
them.

these make a
rich soup.

fill the pot with vege-
tables, cover and cook
fast. Don't add water,
the vegetables do that.
Cook just till it's soupy.
Serve a different soup
each time, each season.

bellies up. Changing winds cause the leaves to flip and the weather to change. Winds from the south or southeast often bring rain in twenty-four hours and if you hear extra noisy crickets, see a red sunrise, no morning dew or a dull gray sunset, you'll get rain soon probably. Thunderheads, which usually develop in the west or northwest, will bring a lollapolooser of a storm, complete with lightning.

Tree Planting

There are several simple rules to remember when planting a tree. If you follow all of them the tree is most likely to survive the shock of a new home.

1. Choose a suitable location for the tree, where it can get its share of good soil, sunshine, and shelter if needed. Don't set it too near other trees. At least the width of the branches away.

2. Dig a ten-dollar hole for a two-dollar tree.

3. The bottom of the hole should be sprinkled with a couple of shovelfuls of compost, leaf mold, or other nutritious natural matter.

4. Keep the roots of the tree shaded and moist until planting. Do not soak. If you cannot plant the tree immediately, lay it on its side and cover the entire root ball with soil.

5. Set tree gently in hole, being careful of the tender roots—they are the tree's most important part.

6. Cover the roots with finely pulverized soil, packing it in gently but firmly to make sure there are no air holes. Add compost as you go along.

7. Bury the roots and the stem of the tree to at least the depth of its original soil; you can see the little ring on the trunk where it used to emerge from the ground.

Once you plant them
they come up every
year.

hollyhock	daffodil	day lily
peony	bleeding heart	phlox
tulip	lily of the valley	poppy
rose	forget-me-not	iris

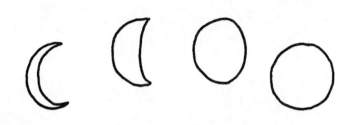

moon planting

1. plants that bear above the ground should be planted in the waxing moon. (When the moon is getting bigger.)

2. plants that bear below the ground, root crops, should be planted in the waning moon. (After the full moon to before the new moon.)

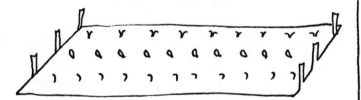

8. Some trees need through watering after being planted. Find out what your tree needs.

9. Put a heavy layer of mulch around the base of the tree. The mulch will keep the soil warm in the fall and cool and moist in the summer.

10. Prune if required. The branches of the tree should be equal to or less than the roots. Pruning is optional.

11. Try to plant the tree on a cloudy day.

12. Find out what season is best for planting in your area. In some places, fall is the best time; in others, spring.

13. Never dig and transplant a tree in midsummer. Only move a tree during its dormant stage, early spring or fall.

Value by the Ton
To determine the value of goods sold by the ton, multiply the number of pounds by the price per ton, point off three places, and divide by two.

Vandals
Petty theft is increasing in the country. Obviously, it's a long long way from the conditions in the city, but you should take reasonable precautions with your house and material things by having good locks on the doors. If you don't live at the farm all year round, avoid storing up liquor, stereos, and other valuables.

Wagon Bed
If it's three feet wide and ten feet long, it will hold two bushels for every inch of depth.

Wallpaper
A standard single roll of wallpaper is 22 inches wide and 252 inches, or 21 feet, long. When you wallpaper over

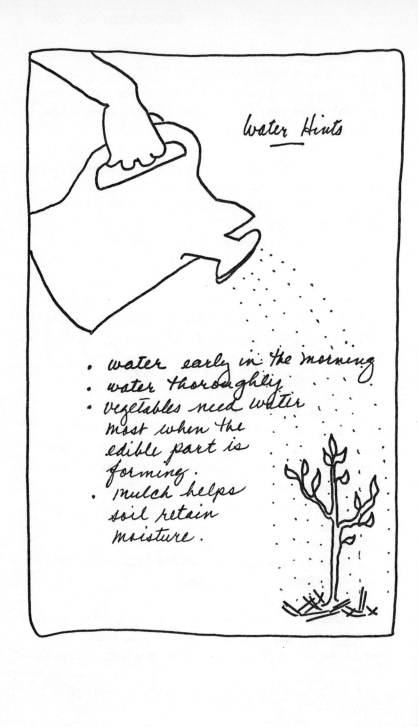

Water Hints

- water early in the morning
- water thoroughly.
- vegetables need water most when the edible part is forming.
- mulch helps soil retain moisture.

old wallpaper, or when you're in doubt as to the newness of plaster on the wall, you should size the wall before you start hanging. If in doubt, size. It's easy, fast, and helps to hold paper on in steamy kitchens, sunny rooms, and in situations where the hanger is new to the subject. A presized wall paste is an acceptable combination of size and paste and if you can find it in country hardware stores, buy it. It saves a step.

Waste Not, Want Not.

Water, In Absentia

If you've planted a tree or any other plant that needs constant moisture to get started; if you're worried about the very hot dry days and their effect on your new plant; here's how to keep it watered when you can't be there with a hose every day. Tote a big barrel out to the spot and punch holes in the lower sides of it. You can leave the barrel on ground level, or you can bury it in the ground up to the top. Then fill it with water and it will drip out just enough to keep the ground moist around your new friend.

Water Pressure

To find the pressure in pounds per square inch at the base of a column of water, a vertical water pipe for instance, multiply the column height in feet by 434.

Water Requirements

Horse	7–10	gallons a day
Cow	6–10	gallons
Hog	2–3	gallons
Sheep	1–2	gallons
100 chickens	5½	gallons

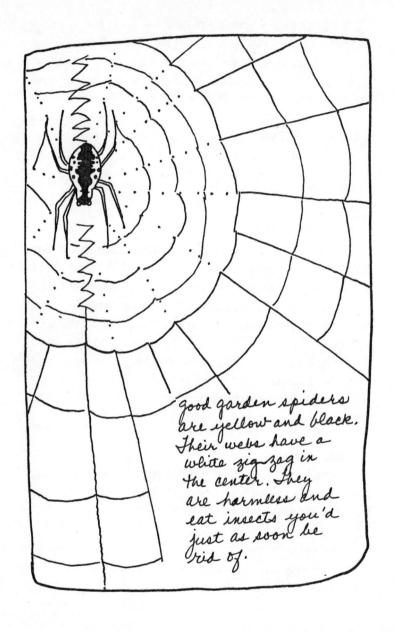

good garden spiders
are yellow and black.
Their webs have a
white zig-zag in
the center. They
are harmless and
eat insects you'd
just as soon be
rid of.

The secret of freezing: fire and ice.

Cook vegetables fast with a hot fire.

Take vegetables out and into icy water after two or three minutes.

Fast cooking saves vitamins.

Fast cooling keeps vegetables crisp.

Windbreaks

Trees can act like air conditioners. When planted in masses, almost like a fence, trees help control soil blowing and reduce the drying effects of wind on soil and plants. If wind erosion is a problem for you, plant trees. If heat is a problem, plant trees. Locate your windbreak perpendicular to the prevailing winds.

Woodpecker

This bird is much maligned. He is in fact a good friend. He eats wood-boring insects, May beetles, weevils, and many other bugs and their larvae. He looks for trees where these insects are likely to be and begins his feast and his tapping. His poor reputation is deserved only because the holes he makes may let fungus spores into the tree and cause it to rot. However, the tree probably had something wrong with it since it harbored so many wood-boring insects to begin with.

Rules for Measurement

To find the diameter of a circle, multiply circumference by .31831.

To find the circumference of a circle, multiply diameter by 3.1416.

To find the area of a circle, multiply square of diameter by .7854.

To find the surface of a ball or sphere, multiply square of diameter by 3.1416.

To find the volume of a ball or sphere, multiply cube of diameter by .5236.

To find the area of a triangle, multiply the perpendicular height by the base and divide by two.

Daylily

You can have an instant garden by planting a few bulbs. The flowers are huge and colorful and the plant spreads year after year.

The buds are good to eat. Cook with a little butter.

How to keep rabbits out of your garden.

1. Sprinkle rock phosphate on seedlings.

2. Sprinkle dried blood around the roots.

3. Plant onions.

4. Put up a poultry fence, 30 inches high. (the above suggested by Rodale's Encyclopedia of Organic Gardening.)

5. Pee around the edges of the garden. Rabbits sometimes will respect your scent.

To find the area of a trapezoid, multiply half of the sum of parallel sides by perpendicular height.

To find the area of an ellipse, multiply long diameter by short diameter by .7854.

To find the area of a parallelogram, multiply base by perpendicular height.

Rectangular Bodies

They are reduced to cubic feet or inches by multiplying the length, width, and height together. Thus a bin 8 feet long 5 feet wide and 4 feet high contains $8 \times 5 \times 4 = 160$ cubic feet.

Cylindrical Bodies

They are reduced to cylinder feet or inches by multiplying the square of the diameter by the depth. They are reduced to cubic feet by multiplying the cylindrical feet by .7854. So a tank, diameter 5 feet, depth 4 feet contains $5^2 \times 4 = 100$ cylindrical feet; and $100 \times .7854 = 78\frac{1}{2}$ cubic feet.

You can measure the height of tall trees or buildings by using a simple system. Set up a stick in the ground and measure its shadow. Then measure the tree's shadow. The height of the tree equals the length of the tree's shadow times the height of the stick divided by the length of the stick's shadow.

Weights and Measures

Commercial Weight

27 11/32 grains	1 dram
16 drams	1 ounce
16 ounces	1 pound
2000 pounds	1 ton
2240 pounds	1 long ton

Some seeds can be planted
before the last frost in the
spring.

early beets   parsnips
broccoli   parsley
early cabbage   peas
carrots   potatoes
head lettuce   radishes
onion   spinach
                   turnips

Dry Measure

2 pints ....1 quart
8 quarts...................1 peck
4 pecks ....1 bushel

Long Measure

12 inches.................1 foot
18 inches.................1 cubit
3 feet (36 inches)......1 yard
16½ feet (5½ yards)..1 rod or pole
40 poles or rods........1 furlong
320 rods (8 furlongs) .1 mile
5280 feet (1760) yards).1 mile
69 1/8 miles..............1 degree

Square Measure

144 square inches......1 square foot
9 square feet ....1 square yard
30¼ square yards ......1 square rod, perch, or pole
272¼ square feet.......1 square rod, perch, or pole
40 square rods ....1 square rood
4 square roods ....1 acre
43,560 square feet .....1 acre
640 acres.................1 square mile

Liquid Measure

4 gills.....................1 pint
2 pints ....1 quart
4 quarts..................1 gallon
31½ gallons ....1 barrel
2 barrels ....1 hogshead

EQUIVALENTS

A pint's a pound the world around. Just about. A pint

of water, wheat, butter, sugar, or blackberries weighs a pound.

One gallon of water weighs about 8 1/3 pounds.

One gallon of milk weighs about 8.6 pounds.

One gallon of cream weighs about 8.4 pounds.

One gallon of kerosene weighs about 6.5 pounds.

One keg of nails weighs 100 pounds.

One horsepower is equal to raising 33,000 pounds 1 foot per minute.

One-third of an inch equals one size in measuring shoes.

Four inches equals one hand in measuring horses.

One board-foot equals 144 cubic inches.